The Abilene Paradox
and Other Meditations
on Management

The Abilene Paradox and Other Meditations on Management

Jerry B. Harvey

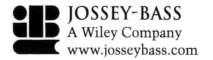

JOSSEY-BASS
A Wiley Company
www.josseybass.com

Published by Jossey-Bass
A Wiley Imprint
989 Market Street, San Francisco, CA 94103-1741   www.josseybass.com

FIRST PAPERBACK EDITION PUBLISHED IN 1996.
THIS BOOK WAS ORIGINALLY PUBLISHED BY LEXINGTON BOOKS.

Chapter 2 is adapted by permission of the publisher, from J. Harvey, "The Abilene Paradox: The Management of Agreement," *Organizational Dynamics*, Summer 1974 © 1974 AMACOM, a division of American Management Associations, New York. All rights reserved.

Chapter 3 is adapted by permission of the publisher, from J. Harvey, "Organizations as Phrog Farms," *Organizational Dynamics*, Spring, 1977 © 1977 AMACOM, a division of American Management Associations, New York. All rights reserved.

Chapter 8 is adapted, by permission of the publisher, from J. Harvey, "Encouraging Students to Cheat: One Thought on the Difference Between Teaching Ethics and Teaching Ethically," *Organizational Behavior Teaching Review* 9(2), 1984. Copyright 1984, all rights reserved and "Learning to Not Teach," *Organizational Behavior Teaching Review* 4(3), 1979. Copyright 1979, all rights reserved.

Readers should be aware that Internet Web sites offered as citations and/or sources for further information may have changed or disappeared between the time this was written and when it is read.

Jossey-Bass books and products are available through most bookstores. To contact Jossey-Bass directly call our Customer Care Department within the U.S. at 800-956-7739, outside the U.S. at 317-572-3986, or fax 317-572-4002.

Jossey-Bass also publishes its books in a variety of electronic formats. Some content that appears in print may not be available in electronic books.

Library of Congress Cataloging-in-Publication Data

Harvey, Jerry B.
    The Abilene paradox and other meditations on
        management.
    Bibliography: p.
    1. Organizational behavior—Moral and ethical
aspects—Anecdotes, facetiae, satire, etc.
    2. Management—Moral and ethical aspects—Anecdotes,
facetiae, satire, etc. I. Title
    ISBN 0–669–19179–5
    ISBN 0–7879–0277–2 (paper)
HD58.7.H376   1988
658'.00207   88–45176

FIRST EDITION
HB Printing   15 14 13 12 11 10 9
PB Printing   15 14 13 12

Contents

Acknowledgments

ALTHOUGH I take full responsibility for the content of these essays-turned-sermons, many others have contributed to them directly and still others have made indirect contributions, the character of which some of the contributors themselves may be unaware. I would like to express my particular appreciation to some of them.

I am grateful to Bill Dyer, a long-time colleague and friend who originally gave me the idea for the book, although I doubt that he remembers doing so. Specifically, he suggested that I put together a collection of my writings so that my children and, as yet, unborn grandchildren might someday understand more about me and what I do for a living than they now do. As I remember, the gist of his recommendation was, "You have always been a little weird, and a compilation of some of your work might help them comprehend your more blatant peculiarities."

Peter Vaill, another colleague and friend, probably has contributed more to the content of the book than anyone other than myself. He has discussed ideas with me, composed memos, written poetry, pasted articles on my door, suggested sources of information, read drafts, and provided encouragement. On several occasions, he has also refused invitations to have his specific contributions formally acknowledged, sometimes with the statement, "Who wants to be associated with that?"

Erik Winslow, John Lobuts, Bill Halal, David Brown, Tony Petrella, Warner Burke, Vlad Dupre, Martha Williams, Ira Iscoe, Jay Hall, Sue Eichhorn, and the late Gordon Lippitt have provided the same sort of good-humored collegiality, friendship, and support.

Albert Gross helped me revise and shorten my initial manuscript so that the final book could attempt to meet the needs of the broadest possible audience of managers. To say that I appreciate the competent care with which he did his work would be a substantial understatement.

Those familiar with my inattention to detail will know how appreciative I am for the competent research and editorial assistance of Cathy Brooks, Connie Bender, Colleen Jones, Sharon Peruzzi Strauchs, and John John.

I also want to offer my thanks to the many students and clients who have contributed to my work over the years.

Regardless of what others have given to it, the book is dedicated with love to Beth, Scott, and Suzanne, who serve as daily reminders that God's love receives expression in the most wonderful human terms.

1

Introduction

M Y DAUGHTER Suzanne has long been the gnostic of our family. For example, shortly after her seventh birthday, she returned from church services and confronted me with the question, "Daddy, what if God is a mouse?"

Being a college professor with a Ph.D. in psychology and having read more than a little in such disciplines as psychiatry, group dynamics, organizational theory, religion, philosophy, and physiology, I feel that I am reasonably well prepared to answer questions that deal with human behavior, management, and comparative theology. For reasons known only to God (or mice), however, I did not feel adequately prepared for Suzanne's metaphysical onslaught. Therefore, trying to maintain the semblance of decorum required of any self-respecting father who doesn't want his daughter to discover early in life that his wing-tip shoes cover feet of clay, I replied with what I thought, under the circumstances, was admirable calmness, "What do you mean, 'What if God is a mouse?'"

"Well," said she, "if God is a mouse, aren't we wasting a lot of time going to church? And even if we do go, shouldn't we be putting cheese in the collection plate? A mouse wouldn't want money."

"Suzanne," I responded, feeling my studious, self-assured facade beginning to crumble, "you can't ask questions like that. You just have to accept the fact that God is God. I mean, you can't bound around the house willy-nilly, questioning the existence of the One Who Put Us Here. You simply have to accept the fact that God exists and go from there."

Then, experiencing a renewed sense of confidence—stemming from her puzzled stare—I went on: "Who do you think made the universe, the stars, the moon, and the planets? Who makes the rain fall and the sun shine? Who makes the grass grow and the seasons change?" Aware that I might be going a little beyond the bounds of philosophic decency, I decided to conclude my discourse with something a little more pragmatic and to the point, at least a point that I was sure a seven-year-old could understand, and said, "Who makes the cocoa beans that make the chocolate that goes into M and M's? Answer that for me."

"Mice, maybe," she replied, totally unfazed. "They are pretty smart. You sure haven't been able to catch the ones in our basement."

I began to feel exasperated. Although related to me because of biology, this little snippet simply could not treat me and God in such cavalier fashion, so I decided to end the debate once and for all.

"Suzanne," her name came out in my most authoritative voice, "I don't want to hear you ever ask again, 'What if God is a mouse?' I don't want you blubbering on about whether God is an orangutan, an armadillo or a potted plant, either. Questioning God's existence is immoral. It's communistic. What if everyone did it? Things would get messed up. Why don't you just drop the whole question and go play hide-and-seek with Megan?"

"Why?" she said. "If God is who He says He is, He wouldn't mind us asking the question; and if He isn't, we sure ought to quit trying to catch the mice downstairs. We might break God's neck in a trap. I think it would be better for us to find out who He is than to smash Him with that spring-like thing you bought at the hardware store." (I am aware that some of you may believe that God is a woman. If so, I suggest that you contact Suzanne directly with your concern. I am sure she would be glad to discuss it with you.)

I don't recall how the conversation concluded. I do have some vague memory of shouting for my wife, Beth, to join the fray. If she did, I don't recollect it. Regardless of the status of my memory, I know that if she did participate, she was of no help; because since that day, in addition to being obsessed with the implications of Suzanne's basic question, I have had a recurring dream, which leaves me sometimes in euphoria and sometimes in terror, of going to church and putting Swiss cheese in the collection plate. Even worse, I have dreamed more than once of wandering into the basement some morning and confronting a massed chorus of grieving rodents who are engaged in singing the dirge "God Is Dead" while gazing at a small mousetrap that holds within its wire jaws the furry little figure of their beloved god, Muridae, whom I killed.

As I have been able to detach myself from the ravages of her penetrating theological foray, I have begun to believe that Suzanne is correct—not about the possibility that God is a mouse, but about our having to ask repeatedly the question, "What if God is a mouse?" After all, when Thomas Merton conducted his *Raids on the Unspeakable*, he concluded, rather sensibly I thought, that arrogance makes tsars out of mice; so I could see no reason that Suzanne couldn't join Merton's raids by asking whether God might exist in the image of a rodent.[1]

Her contention that we must be free to consider such a possibility took on even more meaning for me when I began to put into print some of the ideas, beliefs, thoughts, feelings, and intuitions I have had over the years about issues of organization and the practice of management.

When I showed drafts of my material to a close friend and colleague, Peter Vaill, he responded in a letter: "You are, and I say this caringly, overly disposed to utilize the sermonic form."

At first I was indignant, then outraged, and finally intrigued. In articles such as "The Abilene Paradox"[2] and "Organizations as Phrog Farms,"[3] I had indeed written (albeit unintentionally) in a sermonic form. It is a form that—as Peter Vaill correctly pointed out—is characterized by "The Everyday Story That Means Something Larger." In addition, I have served time as a deacon in a semi-tub-thumping Southern Baptist church, and I have long been deeply concerned with matters ethical and spiritual. Furthermore, on more than one occasion, colleagues, clients, and friends, though unaware of my religious background and convictions, have contended that I sometimes speak with the rhythm and cadence of a fundamentalist tent-revival minister. For those reasons, plus others that undoubtedly reside in my unconscious, I decided to interpret Peter's remark in its best potential light by adding a comment he didn't make: "Why don't you admit that your essays are sermons, call them that, and go on from there?"

Hence, I won't deny my spiritual convictions and predilections. Rather, I have decided to "come out of the closet" and own up to the fact that a part of me has always wanted to take his place in the pulpit.

As I follow current events in commerce and government, I am more confident about my decision to own up to my tendency to sermonize. For instance, the zeitgeist of contemporary American business seems to be dominated by "corporate raiders," who leverage their way into multi-billion-dollar acquisitions and mergers. Often, the raiders destroy the enterprises they acquire by selling off choice pieces to finance the original purchase. Frequently, hard-working, competent managers are summarily dismissed by the raiders for reasons of economy. Loyal, skilled blue-collar workers lose their careers and the means to support their families as entire plants are shut down with callous disregard for the human consequences of decisions made for the short-term benefit of a corporation. In the realm of government, a president and administration that said they would never ever ransom hostages make tawdry arms deals with the Ayatollah's government and then violate the expressed decree of Congress by giving the profits to mercenaries fighting in Central America. Perhaps it is high time that some of us who are interested in managerial behavior voice the ethical and moral questions related to the functioning of American organizations. Therefore, in the "sermons" of this book, I attempt to explore the origins and ethical implications of the moral dilemmas confronting today's managers.

The first issue I broach is the tendency of groups of two or more homo sapiens to take what I call "trips to Abilene." When I first published "The Abilene Paradox," I only wished to use a personal example to illustrate how organizations actually have greater difficulty coping with their supposed agreement than managing their conflict. To my surprise, the article hit a responsive chord. McGraw-Hill made the parable into a management movie; and I frequently hear from some managers who complain that their organizations have taken trips to Abilene and others who describe with delight how they avoided such journeys. People also tell me that the phrase *Abilene*

Paradox has become relatively common management jargon. Obviously, the Abilene Paradox is a more pervasive problem than I initially had believed.

In subsequent chapters, I take up such issues as the alienation in organizations and the tendency of managers to follow orders without questioning authority. I then ask why managerial life prohibits the same contrition and forgiveness that is taken for granted in the religious traditions of most managers. In the chapter entitled "Eichmann in the Organization," I ask whether collusion in organizational holocausts is inevitable. Next, I turn a jaundiced eye toward the widely held assumption that the pressure to conform can explain the group tyranny exemplified by the lynch mob; perhaps that notion is merely an excuse for the irresponsibility of mob members. Finally, I explain that I encourage cheating, because our educational system has penalized the very collaboration we so desperately need to make our organizations productive.

As one might guess, I have some reservations about overtly moralizing on the subject of management. I have been besieged by negative fantasies of the disasters that will befall me if I stray from the management scientist's obsession with the bottom line and worker satisfaction and speak instead of the moral and philosophical implications of organizational behavior. Disturbing to say the least, my fantasies have found expression in such diverse forms as: "I will lose whatever professional status and creditability I have gained over the years;" "My colleagues will ostracize me;" "My consultation practice will suffer;" "Students will no longer sign up for my courses;" "I will appear foolish;" "Readers will not take my work seriously;" and perhaps the most frightening fantasy of all, "Readers *will* take my work seriously." But having read my own sermon, "The Abilene Paradox," in which I attempt to offer some insight about the destructive role of negative fantasies, I realize that the ultimate purpose of such reveries is to provide me with an excuse for avoiding the existential risk that comes from genuinely inquiring into the nature of the world of which I am a part.

Stated differently, as long as I, through the medium of my fantasies, can convince myself and others that I will be damaged or destroyed if I try something that, for me, is new and different and sensible, then I can spare myself the difficult and risky work involved in getting on with the task of coming to grips with the essence of my soul.

I have opted not to give in to those fantasies. Rather, I have chosen to ask, "What if traditional 'management theory' is a mouse?" – particularly when its tenets are applied to the domain of the human psyche (or soul). Furthermore, I have decided to ask, and maybe answer, that question (for me, anyway) in the form of a series of sermons on the topic of organization behavior.

Not only are the chapters in this book sermons, but they are also, at times, tub-thumping, hellfire-and-damnation sermons. As you may or may not know, such sermons are generally passionate, occasionally dogmatic, and universally moralistic. Though delivered primarily from the darkness, the best of them eventually point to the light. They walk a fine line between being disciplined statements of belief and undisciplined harangues. For those reasons and perhaps others, they frequently disturb the comfortable and comfort the disturbed. Some parishioners are irritated and turned off by them. Others are stimulated by and learn from them. Few respond to them neutrally.

Competent sermons of the sort I am describing are not delivered with the intent of convincing anyone to believe anything or do anything. They are offered to the congregation as thoughts that the preacher believes to be important. As Wilfred Bion, a great practitioner of psychoanalytic homiletics, implied, such thoughts – if they are real thoughts rather than nonthoughts, disthoughts, or rethoughts – exist independently of the thinker. All they need is someone who is willing to express them. Once expressed, they become the basis of genuine conversation.[4] I would be delighted if my sermons result in such conversation.

As I wrote about leadership, followership, group dynamics, communication, motivation, morale, productivity, consensus, and cause and effect, I realized that I was not preaching about those concepts in the manner I had long found to be both comfortable and undemanding. I was not communicating in the liturgical style that had served me so well since my days as a novitiate in secular theology at the Department of Psychology of the University of Texas. Once again, though, Suzanne's question – "What if God is a mouse?" – seemed relevant. It seemed relevant because the "old way" has not been very satisfying or productive to me of late. Perhaps I am better off saying whatever I have to say and thinking whatever I have to think in whatever way I do it best, rather than dealing with issues that are of little concern to me in a way I do it worst. Indeed, what if the god that dictates that I write in the dispassionate third-person language of the behavioral science priesthood is a mouse?

Finally, I realize that regardless of my formal professional affiliations as a psychologist, a professor of management science, and a consultant to organizations, I am, at heart, not only a preacher but also a storyteller. I think part of my proclivity and fondness for storytelling came from my maternal grandfather. Clad in drop-seat "bibtuck" overalls, holding an empty half-pound Folger's coffee can that served as a depository for the effluence that poured from the snuff-processing factory located between his jaws, he practiced the art while ensconced in a cane-bottomed rocking chair located on the screened porch of my grandparents' rambling north Texas farmhouse. (Several years ago, after a thirty-year hiatus, I paid a sentimental visit to that vast exemplar of Texas blackland architecture, only to find that it was little more than a tiny, box-shaped, ramshackle, tar-paper shack—a discovery that, to me, just goes to show what a little creative storytelling can do to accomplish what my grandfather used to call "Making the best of a bad *sit-she-a-shun.*")

Whatever the character of the environment in which he spun his yarns, he regaled his five grandchildren with dry, preposterous, hilarious, improbable, sometimes terrifying, occasionally poignant, and generally interminable stories. One was about a catfish that dragged him the full length of the Mississippi River. Another concerned a mule that he trained to sing bass in the church choir.

An all-time favorite of the grandchildren was his description of what happened to one of his neighbors—the rather buxom Mrs. Lenora Thrusher—when, during an unaccountable lapse of concentration, she leaned over the motor-driven wringer of her new electric washing machine and got one (or more) parts of her anatomy temporarily entangled in its workings. I can still remember my grandfather's description of her, perched on the rooftop of her house, clinging to the chimney, shouting to Beecher, her husband, "Get rid of the damn thing before it maims us all."

Equally vivid is the memory of my grandmother chastising him, again and again, "Frank, you shouldn't tell those kids stories like that." Although my grandfather's influence may contribute to a sense of irreverence that some people say makes my sermons palatable for even the staunchest, dyed-in-the-wool atheist, in retrospect, I nearly agree with my grandmother's admonitions. Today, when I hear someone use the trite expression, "I got caught in a wringer," I know all too well — perhaps better than the speaker — the origin of the comment and the earthy reality of its meaning.

Another part of my storytelling proclivity I attribute to my father. He hid an immense sadness and all-encompassing sense of personal defeat with a sense of humor, expressed through stories — most of which correctly placed him at the butt-end of life's jokes. Similar to the self-deprecating comedian Rodney Dangerfield, my father "didn't get no respect." In fact, his work as a demeaned, low-level, undervalued postal clerk killed him many years before we buried him. Unlike Rodney, though, my father was not well paid for the respect he failed to get. About all he got was a son who too late appreciated his courageous capacity to laugh (and help others laugh) through the pain. Through his reluctant sacrifice, he also got a son who has a deep understanding of the bittersweet couplet in "Through The Forest" by Robert Frost:

> *Forgive, O Lord, my little jokes on Thee*
> *And I'll forgive Thy great big one on me.* [5]

Dear Father, I forgive you after all these years. Will you forgive me for my failure to recognize, while you lived, the enormous suffering your laugh-producing stories hid?

Whatever the source of the stories I tell, they are my way of communicating. But the reader should be warned: I tell stories because they help me make sense out of what is frequently an insane and absurd world. I tell them because they are more interesting to me than telling analyses of variance or correlation coefficients. I tell them because they are my expressions of truth. Carl Jung spoke for me in the "Prologue" to *Memories, Dreams, Reflections,* when he said, "I can only make direct statements, only 'tell stories.' Whether or not the stories are 'true' is not the problem. The only question is whether what I tell is my fable, my truth."[6] Thus, although the stories I recount are expressions of the truth as I see it, I won't vouch for their being factual. I do have — as my son Scott has pointed out on more than one occasion — a tendency to "elaborate a bit."

As I muse about this collection of sermons, some of which I have created and some of which have created me, I realize that the essence of my attitude about and orientation to them is captured in a story one of my graduate students told me immediately after the conclusion of the investigation into what is now termed, "The Watergate Conspiracy."

The student had been employed as a lawyer in the White House, working for one of the principals in the debacle — one who was later convicted and sent to prison for his role in that sordid affair. According to my student friend, he and other lawyers working for the principal were frequently asked to participate in immoral and illegal activities, even prior to Watergate. If they balked at carrying out such activities, they received an Orwellian lecture from their superior as to why what they knew to be immoral and illegal was, in reality, moral and legal. Furthermore, if they carried out the task competently, they were rewarded with pay increases, "perks," and closer access to the center of power. Anyway, as a defense against the pain generated by their moral complicity, they developed an in-house joke that went as follows:

A young man was graduated from Harvard Law School and went to Washington to make his mark on Washington society. He joined a prestigious law firm and began to work twenty hours a day, seven days a week, in the hope of being made a senior partner.

After about six months of working under intense pressure at such a pace, he was approached by one of the senior partners, who said, "We have noticed your work. If you continue at the same pace and produce the same quality of work, we are going to consider making you a partner." So for six months, twenty hours a day, seven days a week, the young man labored in the vineyard of law, in anticipation of his just reward.

However, one Sunday evening at midnight, he decided he would leave the office early and surprise his long-suffering wife. As he drove into the driveway of his split-level suburban home, he noticed a Cadillac in the driveway. He parked his car quietly, turned off the motor, and headed toward his house. He went through the back door, found no one in the kitchen, dining room, or family area, but noticed a light shining beneath the door of the upstairs bedroom.

He took off his shoes so as to reduce the noise, crept up the stairs, slowly opened the bedroom door, and peeked through the unobtrusive crack, only to see his wife and the senior partner engaged in what one might euphemistically term "amorous activities of the first magnitude."

He quietly closed the door, tiptoed down the stairs, silently slipped out the back door, pushed his car into the street so it would make little noise when he started it, carefully cranked the motor, slowly drove to the corner, "floor-boarded" the foot-pedal, and raced at sixty miles an hour through the deserted streets toward his law office.

He reached his office building, brought the car to a sliding halt, and forgetting to turn off the headlights, rushed to the elevator. The elevator was locked for the night, so he darted for the stairway, sped up eight flights of stairs two at a time, burst into his office, rushed to his desk, collapsed in the security of his leather-backed chair, cradled his head in his hands, and gasped, "My God! I nearly got caught."

To me, the theory and practice of organization and management frequently reflects the same essential convoluted thought process. Consequently, unless we can question its basic assumptions, discuss it from the point of view of different premises, and communicate what we know in methods other than those prescribed by the high priests of logical positivism — in short, unless we can ask, "What if God is a mouse?" — then each of us runs the metaphorical risk of living our lives in quiet desperation, trapped in decaying organizations, sitting at our places of work, heads cradled in our hands, munching cheese, and periodically muttering, "My God! I nearly got caught"—knowing full well that mouse gods also make men (and women) in their own images.

This book is a chronicle of some of my efforts during the past fifteen years or so to avoid that trap. Perhaps it will assist you in doing the same.

2

The Abilene Paradox:
The Management of Agreement

T HAT July afternoon in Coleman, Texas (population 5,607), was particularly hot – 104 degrees according to the Walgreen's Rexall's thermometer. In addition, the wind was blowing fine-grained West Texas topsoil through the house. But the afternoon was still tolerable – even potentially enjoyable. A fan was stirring the air on the back porch; there was cold lemonade; and finally, there was entertainment. Dominoes. Perfect for the conditions. The game requires little more physical exertion than an occasional mumbled comment, "Shuffle 'em," and an unhurried movement of the arm to place the tiles in their appropriate positions on the table. All in all, it had the makings of an agreeable Sunday afternoon in Coleman. That is, until my father-in-law suddenly said, "Let's get in the car and go to Abilene and have dinner at the cafeteria."

I thought, "What, go to Abilene? Fifty-three miles? In this dust storm and heat? And in an unairconditioned 1958 Buick?"

But my wife chimed in with, "Sounds like a great idea. I'd like to go. How about you, Jerry?" Since my own preferences were obviously out of step with the rest, I replied, "Sounds good to me," and added, "I just hope your mother wants to go."

"Of course I want to go," said my mother-in-law. "I haven't been to Abilene in a long time."

So into the car and off to Abilene we went. My predictions were fulfilled. The heat was brutal. Perspiration had cemented a fine layer of dust to our skin by the time we arrived. The cafeteria's food could serve as a first-rate prop in an antacid commercial.

Some four hours and 106 miles later, we returned to Coleman, hot and exhausted. We silently sat in front of the fan for a long time. Then, to be sociable and to break the silence, I dishonestly said, "It was a great trip, wasn't it?"

No one spoke.

Finally, my mother-in-law said, with some irritation, "Well, to tell the truth, I really didn't enjoy it much and would rather have stayed here. I just went along because the three of you were so enthusiastic about going. I wouldn't have gone if you all hadn't pressured me into it."

I couldn't believe it. "What do you mean 'you all'?" I said. "Don't put me in the 'you all' group. I was delighted to be doing what we were doing. I didn't want to go. I only went to satisfy the rest of you. You're the culprits."

My wife looked shocked. "Don't call me a culprit. You and Daddy and Mama were the ones who wanted to go. I just went along to keep you happy. I would have had to be crazy to want to go out in heat like that."

Her father entered the conversation with one word: "Shee-it."[a] He then expanded on what was already absolutely clear: "Listen, I never wanted to go to Abilene. I just thought you might be bored. You visit so seldom I wanted to be sure you enjoyed it. I would have preferred to play another game of dominoes and eat the leftovers in the icebox."

After the outburst of recrimination, we all sat back in silence. Here we were, four reasonably sensible people who — of our own volition — had just taken a 106-mile trip across a godforsaken desert in furnace-like heat and a dust storm to eat unpalatable food at a hole-in-the-wall cafeteria in Abilene, when none of us had really wanted to go. To be concise, we'd done just the opposite of what we wanted to do. The whole situation simply didn't make sense.

---

[a]See Larry McMurtry's book, *In a Narrow Grave* (Austin, Tex.: Encino Press, 1968), for an explanation of why Texans rely on scatology when experiencing stress. In the original version of this chapter, published in *Organizational Dynamics*, the word "hell" was substituted. The substitution occurred because the editor and I shared a negative fantasy that our reputations, the credibility of the journal, and the morality of its subscribers would be irreparably damaged by such straightforward Texas terminology.

At least it didn't make sense at the time. But since that day in Coleman, I have observed, consulted with, and been a part of more than one organization that has been caught in the same situation. As a result, the organizations have either taken side trips or, occasionally, terminal "journeys to Abilene," when Dallas or Houston or Tokyo was where they really wanted to go. And for most of those organizations, the negative consequences of such trips, measured in terms of both human misery and economic loss, have been much greater than for our little Abilene group.

I now call the tendency for groups to embark on excursions that no group member wants "the Abilene Paradox." Stated simply, when organizations blunder into the Abilene Paradox, they take actions in contradiction to what they really want to do and therefore defeat the very purposes they are trying to achieve. Business theorists typically believe that managing conflict is one of the greatest challenges faced by any organization, but a corollary of the Abilene Paradox states that the inability to manage *agreement* may be the major source of organization dysfunction. Therefore, in this book I want to suggest ways that organizations can cope more effectively with the pernicious influence of the paradox.

As a means to accomplish this goal, in this sermon I shall describe the symptoms exhibited by organizations caught in the paradox; describe—in abbreviated case studies—how the symptoms occur in a variety of organizations; discuss the underlying causal dynamics; indicate some of the implications of accepting this model for describing organizational behavior; make recommendations for coping with the paradox; and, in conclusion, relate the paradox to a broader existential issue.

Symptoms of the Paradox

The inability to manage agreement—not the inability to manage conflict—is the essential symptom that defines organizations caught in the web of the Abilene Paradox. Groups that fail to manage agreement effectively display six specific characteristics, all of which were present when my family went to Abilene:

1.   Organization members individually agree in private about the nature of the situation or problem facing the organization. For example, members of the Abilene group agreed that they were enjoying themselves sitting in front of the fan, sipping lemonade, and playing dominoes.

2.   Organization members individually agree in private about what steps would be required to cope with the situation or problem. For members of the Abilene group, "more of the same" was a solution that would have adequately satisfied individual and collective desires.

3.   Organization members fail to accurately communicate their desires and/or beliefs to one another. In fact, they do just the opposite, thereby leading one another into misperceiving the collective reality. On the basis of incorrect assumptions about the consensus, each member of the Abilene group communicated inaccurate data to the other members of the organization. The data, in effect, said, "Yeah, it's a great idea. Let's go to Abilene," when, in reality, members of the organization individually and collectively preferred to stay in Coleman.

4.   With such invalid and inaccurate information, organization members make collective decisions that lead them to take actions contrary to what they want to do, thereby arriving at results that are counterproductive to the organization's intent and purposes. Thus, the Abilene group went to Abilene when it preferred to do something else.

5.   As a result of taking actions that are counterproductive, organization members experience frustration, anger, irritation, and dissatisfaction with their organization. Consequently, they form subgroups with trusted acquaintances and blame other subgroups for the organization's dilemma. Frequently, they also blame authority figures and one another. Such phenomena were illustrated in the Abilene group by the "culprit" argument that occurred when we had returned to the comfort of the fan.

6.   Finally, if organization members do not deal with the generic issue—the inability to manage agreement—the cycle repeats itself with greater intensity. Largely because it became conscious of the process, the Abilene group did not reach that point.

To repeat, the Abilene Paradox reflects a failure to manage agreement. In fact, it is my contention that the inability to cope with (manage) agreement, rather than the inability to cope with (manage) conflict, is the single most pressing issue of modern organizations.

Other Trips to Abilene

The Abilene Paradox respects no individuals, organizations, or institutions. Consider two other "trips to Abilene" that illustrate both the pervasiveness of the paradox and its underlying dynamics.

Case 1: The Boardroom

The Ozyx Corporation is a relatively small industrial company that has embarked on a trip to Abilene. The president of Ozyx has hired a consultant to help discover the reasons for the poor profit picture of the company in general and the low morale and productivity of the R&D division in particular. During the process of investigation, the consultant becomes interested in a research project in which the company has invested a sizable proportion of its R&D budget.

When the consultant privately and separately asks the president, the vice-president for research, and the research manager, each describes the project as an idea that looked great on paper but will ultimately fail because of the unavailability of the technology required to make it work. Each of them also acknowledges that continued support of the project will create cash-flow problems that will jeopardize the very existence of the total organization.

Furthermore, each individual indicates that he has not told the others about his reservations. When asked why, the president says that he can't reveal his "true" feelings because abandoning the widely publicized project would make the company look bad in the press. In addition, candor on this issue would probably cause his vice-president's ulcer to kick up or, perhaps, even cause him to quit, "because he has staked his professional reputation on the project's success."

Similarly, the vice-president for research says that he can't let the president or the research manager know of his reservations because the president is so committed to it that "I would probably get fired for insubordination if I questioned the project."

Finally, the research manager says that he can't let the president or vice-president know of his doubts about the project because of their extreme commitment to the project's success.

All indicate that, in meetings with one another, they try to maintain an optimistic facade so that the others won't worry unduly about the project. The research director, in particular, admits to writing ambiguous progress reports so that the president and the vice-president can "interpret them to suit themselves." In fact, he says that he tends to slant them to the "positive" side, "given how committed the brass are."

The scent of the Abilene trail wafts from a paneled conference room where the project research budget is being considered for the following fiscal year. In the meeting itself, praises are heaped on the questionable project, and a unanimous decision is made to continue it for yet another year. This organization has boarded a bus to Abilene.

Although the real issue of agreement finally was confronted only eight months after the bus departed, that was nearly too late. The organization failed to meet a payroll and underwent a two-year period of personnel cutbacks, retrenchments, and austerity. Morale suffered, the most competent technical personnel resigned, and the organization's prestige in the industry declined.

Case 2: Watergate

"Apart from the grave question of who did what, Watergate presents America with the profound puzzle of why," says a May 27, 1973, editorial in the *Washington Star and Daily News.*[1] The editor asks, "What is it that led such a wide assortment of men, many of them high public officials, possibly including the president himself, either to instigate or to go along with and later try to hide a pattern of behavior that by now appears not only reprehensible, but stupid?"

Perhaps a probe of the dynamics of the Abilene Paradox could answer the editor's question. However, I shall let readers reach their own conclusions on the basis of excerpts from testimony before the Senate investigating committee on "the Watergate Affair."

In one exchange, Senator Howard Baker asked Herbert Porter, then a member of the White House staff, why he (Porter) found himself "in charge of or deeply involved in a dirty tricks operation of the campaign." In response, Porter indicated that he had experienced qualms about what he was doing, but that he "was not one to stand up in a meeting and say that this should be stopped. . . . I kind of drifted along."

And when asked by Baker why he had "drifted along," Porter replied, "In all honesty, because of the fear of the group pressure that would ensue, of not being a team player . . . " and "I felt a deep sense of loyalty to him [the president] or was appealed to on that basis."[2]

Jeb Magruder gave a similar response to a question posed by committee counsel Dash. Specifically, when asked about his, Mr. Dean's, and Mr. Mitchell's reactions to Mr. Liddy's proposal, which included bugging the Watergate, Mr. Magruder replied, "I think all three of us were appalled. The scope and size of the project were something that, at least in my mind, were not envisioned. I do not think it was in Mr. Mitchell's mind or Mr. Dean's, although I can't comment on their states of mind at that time." Mr. Mitchell, in his understated way of dealing with such difficult problems, indicated that this was not an "acceptable project."[3]

Later in his testimony, Mr. Magruder said, "I think I can honestly say that no one was particularly overwhelmed with the project. But I think we felt that this information could be useful, and Mr. Mitchell agreed to approve the project, and I then notified the parties of Mr. Mitchell's approval."[4]

Although I obviously was not privy to the private conversations of the principal characters, the data seem to reflect the essential elements of the Abilene Paradox. First, they indicate agreement. Evidently, Mitchell, Porter, Dean, and Magruder agreed that the plan was inappropriate. ("I think I can honestly say that no one was particularly overwhelmed with the project.") Second, the data indicate that the principal figures then proceeded to implement the plan in contradiction to their shared agreement. Third, the data surrounding the case clearly indicate that the plan multiplied the organization's problems rather than solving them. And finally, the organization broke into subgroups, with the various principals—such as the president, Mitchell, Porter, Dean, and Magruder—blaming one another for the dilemma in which they found themselves, and internecine warfare ensued.

In summary, it is possible that because of the inability of White House staff members to cope with the fact that they agreed, the organization took a trip to Abilene.

Analyzing the Paradox

The Abilene Paradox has been stated succinctly as follows: Organizations frequently take actions in contradiction to the data they have for dealing with problems and, as a result, compound their problems rather than solving them. Like all paradoxes, the Abilene Paradox deals with absurdity. On the surface, it makes little sense for organizations—whether they are couples or companies, bureaucracies or governments—to take actions that are diametrically opposed to the data they possess for solving crucial organizational problems. Such actions are particularly absurd because they compound the very problems they are designed to solve, thereby defeating the purposes the organization is trying to achieve. However, as Anatol Rapaport and others have so cogently expressed it, paradoxes are generally paradoxes only because they are based on a logic or rationale that is different from what we understand or expect.[5]

Discovering the aberrant logic not only destroys the paradoxical quality but also offers alternative ways for coping with similar situations. Therefore, part of the dilemma facing an Abilene-bound organization may be the lack of a map—a theory or model—that provides rationality to the paradox.

Let us see if we can create such a map. The map will be developed by examining the underlying psychological themes of the profit-making organization and the bureaucracy, and it will include the following landmarks: (1) action anxiety, (2) negative fantasies, (3) real risk, (4) separation anxiety, and (5) the psychological reversal of risk and certainty. I hope that the discussion of such landmarks will provide harried organization travelers with a new map that will assist them in arriving at where they really want to go and, in addition, will help them assess the risks that are an inevitable part of the journey.

Action Anxiety

The concept of action anxiety provides the first landmark for locating roadways to bypass Abilene. Organization members take actions in contradiction to their understanding of the organization's problems, because thinking about acting in accordance with what they believe needs to be done makes them intensely anxious. Anxiety about following reasonable instincts is caused by factors that will be explored as the other landmarks are described. As a result of action anxiety, decision makers opt to pursue an unworkable research project or participate in an illegal activity rather than acting in a manner congruent with their beliefs. In essence, they choose to endure the negative professional and economic consequences of their decisions in order to avoid such anxiety. It's not that organization members are ignorant—they do know what needs to be done. For example, the principals of the research organization knew they were working on a project that had no real possibility of succeeding. And the central figures of the Watergate episode apparently knew that, for a variety of reasons, the plan to bug the Watergate did not make sense.

Such action anxiety experienced by the various protagonists may not make sense to those of us who are not directly involved, but the dilemma is not a new one. In fact, it is very similar to the anxiety eloquently expressed in Hamlet's famous soliloquy.

It is easy to translate Hamlet's anxious lament into that of the research manager of our R&D organization as he contemplates his report at the budget committee meeting. It might go something like this:

To maintain my sense of integrity and self-worth or compromise it, that is the question. Whether 'tis nobler in the mind to suffer the ignominy that comes from managing a nonsensical research project, or the fear and anxiety that come from making a report the president and V.P. may not like to hear.

So the anguish, procrastination, and counterproductive behavior of the research manager or of members of the White House staff are not much different from those of Hamlet; all might ask with equal justification Hamlet's subsequent searching question of what it is that "makes us rather bear those ills we have than fly to others we know not of."[6]

In short, like the various Abilene protagonists, we are faced with a deeper question: Why does action anxiety occur?

Negative Fantasies

Part of the answer to that question may be found in the negative fantasies organization members have about acting in congruence with what they believe should be done.

Hamlet experienced such fantasies. Specifically, Hamlet's fantasies of the alternatives to current evils were more evils, and he didn't entertain the possibility that any action he might take could lead to an improvement in the situation. Hamlet's was not an unusual case, though. In fact, the "Hamlet syndrome" clearly occurred in both the industrial company and the Nixon White House. All of the organization protagonists had negative fantasies about what would happen if they acted in accordance with what they believed needed to be done.

The various managers in the R&D organization foresaw loss of face, prestige, position, and even health as the outcome of confronting the issues about which they believed, incorrectly, that they disagreed. Similarly, members of the White House staff feared being made scapegoats, branded as disloyal, or ostracized as non-team players if they acted in accordance with their understanding of reality.

To sum up, action anxiety is partly caused by the negative fantasies that organization members have about what will happen if they act in accordance with their understanding of what is sensible. The negative fantasies, in turn, serve an important function for the persons who have them. Specifically, they provide the individual with an excuse that releases him psychologically—both in his own eyes and, frequently, in the eyes of others—from the responsibility of having to act to solve organization problems.

It is not sufficient, though, to stop with the explanation of negative fantasies as the basis for the inability of organizations to cope with agreement. We must look deeper and ask still other questions: What is the source of the negative fantasies? Why do they occur?

Real Risk

Risk is a reality of life, a condition of existence. John Kennedy articulated it in another way when he said at a news conference, "Life is unfair." By that I believe he meant to say that we do not know, nor can we predict or control with certainty, either the events that impinge upon us or the outcomes of actions we undertake in response to those events.

Consequently, in the business environment, the research manager might find that telling the president and the vice-president that the project was a "turkey" might result in his being fired. And Mr. Porter may have been ostracized as a non-team player for saying that an illegal plan of surveillance should not be carried out. There are too many cases in which confrontation of this sort has resulted in such consequences. The real question, though, is not "Are such fantasized consequences possible?" but "Are such fantasized consequences likely?"

Thus, real risk is an existential condition. All actions have consequences that—to paraphrase Hamlet—may be worse than the evils of the present. However, as a result of their unwillingness to accept existential risk as one of life's givens, people may opt to take their organizations to Abilene rather than run the risk—no matter how small—of ending up somewhere worse.

Again, though, one must ask: What is the real risk that underlies the decision to opt for Abilene? What is at the core of the paradox?

Fear of Separation

It is tempting to say that the core of the paradox lies in the individual's fear of the unknown. Actually, however, we do not fear what is unknown, but we *are* afraid of things we do know about. What do we know about that frightens us into such apparently inexplicable organizational behavior?

Separation, alienation, and loneliness are things we do know about—and so is fear. Both research and experience indicate that ostracism is one of the most powerful punishments that can be devised. Solitary confinement does not draw its coercive strength from physical deprivation. The evidence is overwhelming that we have a fundamental need to be connected, engaged, and related and a reciprocal need not to be separated or alone. Every one of us, though, has experienced aloneness. From the time the umbilical cord was cut, we have experienced the real anguish of separation—broken friendships, divorces, deaths, and exclusions. C.P. Snow vividly described the tragic interplay between loneliness and connection:

> Each of us is alone; sometimes we escape from our solitariness, through love and affection or perhaps creative moments, but these triumphs of life are pools of light we make for ourselves while the edge of the road is black. Each of us dies alone.[7]

The fear of taking risks that may result in our separation from others is at the core of the paradox. It finds expression in ways of which we may be unaware, and it is ultimately the cause of the self-defeating, collective deception that leads to self-destructive decisions within organizations.

Concretely, such fear of separation leads research committees to fund projects that none of its members want and, perhaps, leads White House staff members to engage in illegal activities that they don't really support.

The Psychological Reversal of Risk and Certainty

One landmark of the map is still missing. It relates to the peculiar reversal that occurs in our thought processes as we try to cope with the Abilene Paradox. For example, we frequently fail to take action in an organizational setting because we fear that the actions we take may result in our separation from others, or, in the language of Mr.

Porter, because we are afraid of being tabbed as "disloyal" or being ostracized as "non–team players." But therein lies a paradox within a paradox, because our very unwillingness to take such risks virtually ensures the separation and aloneness we so fear. In effect, we reverse real existential risk and fantasied risk and by doing so transform a probability statement into what, for all practical purposes, becomes a certainty.

Take the R&D organization described earlier. When the project fails, some people will get fired, demoted, or sentenced to the purgatory of a make-work job in an out-of-the-way office. For those who remain, the atmosphere of blame, distrust, suspicion, and backbiting that accompanies such failure will serve only to further alienate and separate them.

The Watergate situation is similar. The principals evidently feared being ostracized as disloyal non–team players. When the illegality of the act surfaced, however, it was nearly inevitable that blaming, self-protective actions and scapegoating would result in the very emotional separation from both the president and one another that the principals feared. Thus, by reversing real and fantasied risk, they effectively had ensured the outcome they least desired.

One final question remains: Why do we make this peculiar reversal? I support the general thesis of Alvin Toffler and Philip Slater, who contend that our cultural emphasis on technology, competition, individualism, temporariness, and mobility has resulted in a population that has frequently experienced the terror of loneliness and seldom the satisfaction of engagement. Consequently, though we have learned of the reality of separation, we have not had the opportunity to learn the reciprocal skills of connection, with the result that, like the ancient dinosaurs, we are breeding organizations with self-destructive decision-making proclivities.

A Possible Abilene Bypass

Existential risk is inherent in living, so it is impossible to provide a map that meets the no-risk criterion. But it may be possible to describe the route in terms that make the landmarks understandable and that will clarify the risks involved. In order to do that, however, some commonly used terms—such as *victim, victimizer, collusion, responsibility, conflict, conformity, courage, confrontation, reality,* and *knowledge*—have to be redefined. In addition, we need to explore the relevance of the redefined concepts for bypassing or getting out of Abilene.

Victim and Victimizer. Blaming and fault-finding behavior is one of the basic symptoms of organizations that have found their way to Abilene, and those who criticize generally don't include themselves as targets of blame. In other words, executives begin to assign one another to the roles of victims and victimizers. Ironic as it may seem, however, this assignment of roles is both irrelevant and dysfunctional, because once a business or a government fails to manage its agreement and arrives in Abilene, all of its members are victims. Thus, arguments and accusations that identify victims and victimizers, at best, become symptoms of the paradox, and, at worst, drain energy from the problem-solving efforts required to redirect the organization along the route it really wants to take.

Collusion. A basic implication of the Abilene Paradox is that human problems of organization are reciprocal in nature. As Robert Tannenbaum has pointed out, you can't have an autocratic boss unless subordinates are willing to collude with his autocracy, and you can't have obsequious subordinates unless the boss is willing to collude with their obsequiousness.[8]

Thus, in plain terms, each person in a self-defeating, Abilene-bound organization consciously or unconsciously colludes with others—peers, superiors, and subordinates—to create the dilemma in which the organization finds itself. To adapt a cliché about modern organizations: "It takes a real team effort to go to Abilene." In that sense, each person, in his own collusive manner, shares responsibility for the trip. Hence, searching for a locus of blame outside oneself serves no useful purpose for either the organization or the individual. It neither helps the organization handle its dilemma of unrecognized agreement nor provides psychological relief for the individual, because focusing on conflict when agreement is the issue is devoid of reality. Far from providing relief, the orgy of blaming causes the organization to focus on managing conflict when it should be focusing on managing agreement.

Responsibility for Problem-Solving Action. Who is responsible for getting us out of this place? To that question is frequently appended another rhetorical "should" question: Isn't it the boss—or the ranking government official—who is responsible for doing something about the situation?

The answer to the second question is no. The key to understanding why the "no" answer is functional is the knowledge that, when the dynamics of the paradox are in operation, the authority figure and others are in unknowing agreement with one another concerning the organization's problems and the steps necessary to solve them. Consequently, the power to destroy the pernicious influence of the paradox comes from confronting and addressing the underlying reality of the situation, not from one's hierarchical position within the organization. Therefore, any organization member who chooses to risk confronting that reality possesses the necessary leverage to release the organization from the grip of the paradox.

In one situation, salvation may require a research director to say, "I don't think this project can succeed." In another, it may be Jeb Magruder's response to this question of Senator Baker:

> If you were concerned because the action was known to you to be illegal, because you thought it improper or unethical, you thought the prospects for success were very meager, and you doubted the reliability of Mr. Liddy, what on earth would it have taken to decide against the plan?

Magruder's reply was brief and to the point:

> Not very much, sir. I am sure that if I had fought vigorously against it, I think any of us could have had the plan cancelled.

Reality, Knowledge, and Confrontation. Accepting the paradox as a model that describes certain organizational dilemmas also requires re-thinking the nature of reality and knowledge as they are generally described in organizations. In brief, the underlying dynamics of the paradox clearly indicate that organization members generally know more about issues confronting the organization than they don't know. The various principals attending the research budget meeting, for example, knew that the research project was doomed to failure. And Jeb Magruder spoke as a true Abilener when he said, "We knew it was illegal, probably, inappropriate."[9]

Given this concept of reality and its relationship to knowledge, confrontation becomes the process of facing issues squarely, openly, and directly in an effort to discover whether the nature of the underlying collective reality is agreement or conflict. Accepting such a definition of confrontation has an important implication for change agents who are interested in making organizations more effective. That is, organizational change and effectiveness may be facilitated as much by confronting the organization with what it knows and agrees upon as by confronting it with what it doesn't know or disagrees about.

Real Conflict and Phony Conflict

Conflict is a part of any organizational relationship. Couples, R&D divisions, and White House staffs all engage in it. However, analysis of the Abilene Paradox opens up the possibility of two kinds of conflict—real and phony. On the surface, the two types of conflict look alike, but—like varieties of headache—they have different causes and therefore require different treatment.

Real conflict occurs when people have real differences: "My reading of the research printouts says that we can make the project profitable" versus "I come to the opposite conclusion" or "I suggest we 'bug' the Watergate" versus "I'm not in favor of it."

Phony conflict occurs in the Abilene Paradox because people agree on the actions they want to take and then do the opposite. The resulting anger, frustration, and scapegoating—generally termed *conflict*—are not based on real differences. Rather, they stem from the protective reactions that occur when a decision that no one believed in or was committed to in the first place goes sour. In fact, as a paradox within a paradox, such conflict is symptomatic of agreement!

Group Tyranny and Conformity

An understanding of the dynamics of the Abilene Paradox also requires a reorientation in thinking about concepts such as "group tyranny" – the loss of the individual's distinctiveness in a group and the impact of conformity pressures on individual behavior in organizations.

Group tyranny and its result, individual conformity, generally refer to the coercive effect of group pressures on individual behavior. Sometimes referred to as "groupthink," it has been damned as the cause for everything from the lack of creativity in organizations ("A camel is a horse designed by a committee") to antisocial behavior in juveniles ("My Johnny is a good boy; he was just pressured into shoplifting by the kids he runs around with").

However, an analysis of the dynamics underlying the Abilene Paradox opens up the possibility that individuals frequently feel as if they are experiencing coercive organizational pressures to conform when they actually are responding to the dynamics of mismanaged agreement. Conceptualizing, experiencing, and responding to such experiences as reflecting the tyrannical pressures of a group again serves an important psychological use for the individual: As noted previously, it releases the person from the responsibility of taking action and thus becomes a defense against action. Thus, much behavior within an organization that heretofore has been conceptualized as reflecting the tyranny of conformity pressures is really an expression of collective anxiety and therefore must be reconceptualized as a defense against acting.

In a later chapter, I will deal fully with an American myth that provides an excellent example of such faulty conceptualization. The myth involves the heroic sheriff in the classic Western movie who stands alone in the jail-house door and singlehandedly protects a suspected (and usually innocent) horsethief or murderer from the irrational, tyrannical forces of group behavior—that is, an armed lynch mob. Generally, as a part of the ritual, he threatens to blow off the head of anyone who takes a step toward the door. Few ever take the challenge, and the reason is not the sheriff's six-shooter. What good would one pistol be against an armed mob of several hundred people who really want to hang somebody? Thus, the gun, in fact, serves as a face-saving measure for people who don't wish to participate in a hanging anyway. ("We had to back off. The sheriff threatened to blow our heads off.")

The situation is one that involves agreement management. A careful investigator canvassing the crowd under conditions in which the anonymity of the interviewees' responses could be guaranteed would probably find (1) that few of the individuals in the crowd really wanted to take part in the hanging; (2) that each person's participation came about because he perceived, falsely, that others wanted to do so; and (3) that each person was afraid that others in the crowd would ostracize or in some other way punish him if he did not go along.

Diagnosing the Paradox

Most individuals like quick, "clean," "no-risk" solutions to organizational problems. Furthermore, they tend to prefer solutions based on mechanics and technology, rather than on attitudes of "being." Unfortunately, the underlying reality of the paradox makes it impossible to provide either no-risk solutions or action technologies that are divorced from existential attitudes and realities. I do, however, have two sets of suggestions for dealing with these situations. One set relates to diagnosing the situation, the other to confronting it.

When faced with the possibility that the paradox is operating, one must first make a diagnosis of the situation, and the key to diagnosis is an answer to the question: Is the organization involved in a conflict-management or an agreement-management situation? As an organization member, I have found it relatively easy to make a preliminary diagnosis of whether an organization is on the way to Abilene or is involved in legitimate, substantive conflict by responding to the organization diagnostic survey shown in the box on page 31. If the response to the first statement is "not characteristic," the organization is probably not in Abilene or in conflict. If the response is "characteristic," the organization has a problem of either real or phony conflict, and the responses to the succeeding statements will help determine which it is.

In brief, for reasons that should be apparent from the theory discussed here, the more times the response is "characteristic," the more likely that the organization is on its way to Abilene. In practical terms, a process for managing agreement is the required remedy. Finally, if the response to the first statement falls into the "characteristic" category and most of the other responses fall into the "not characteristic" category, one may be relatively sure that the organization is in a real conflict situation and that some sort of conflict management is in order.

Organization Diagnostic Survey

Instructions: For each of the following statements, please indicate whether it is or is not characteristic of your organization.

1. There is conflict in the organization.
2. Organization members feel frustrated, impotent, and unhappy when trying to deal with it. Many are looking for ways to escape. They may avoid meetings at which the conflict is discussed, they may be looking for new jobs, or they may spend as much time away from the office as possible by taking unneeded trips or vacations or sick leave.
3. Organization members place much of the blame for the dilemma on the boss or other groups. In "back-room" conversations among friends, the boss is termed incompetent, ineffective, "out of touch," or a candidate for early retirement. Nothing is said to his face, or at best, only oblique references are made concerning his role in the organization's problems. If the boss isn't blamed, some other group, division, or unit is seen as the culprit:

We would do fine if it were not for the damn fools in Division X."

4. Small subgroups of trusted friends and associates meet informally over coffee, lunch, and so on, to discuss organizational problems. There is a lot of agreement among the members of these subgroups regarding the cause of the troubles and the solutions that would be effective in solving them. Such conversations are frequently punctuated with statements beginning with "We should do . . . "

5. In meetings where those same people meet with members of other subgroups to discuss the problem, they "soften" their positions, state them in ambiguous language, or even reverse them to suit the apparent positions taken by others.

6. After such meetings, members complain to trusted associates that they really didn't say what they wanted to say, but they also provide a list of convincing reasons why the comments, suggestions, and reactions they wanted to make would have been impossible. Trusted associates commiserate and say that the same was true for them.

7. Attempts to solve the problem do not seem to work. In fact, such attempts seem to add to the problem or make it worse.

8. Individuals seem to get along better, be happier, and operate more effectively outside the organization than they do within it.

Coping with the Paradox

Assuming that a preliminary diagnosis indicates that an organization is on the way to Abilene, the individual organization member may choose to confront the situation actively to determine directly whether the underlying reality is agreement or conflict. The confrontation probably will be most effective if it occurs in a group setting. Working within the context of a group is important, because the dynamics of the Abilene Paradox involve collusion among group members. Therefore, trying to solve the dilemma by working with individuals and small subgroups would involve further collusion and repetition of the dynamics that led to the paradox. The basic approach involves gathering together organization members who are key figures in both the problem and its solution.

The first step in the meeting is for the individual who called the meeting—that is, the confronter—to own up to his or her position first and be open to the consequent feedback. The owning-up process lets the others know that the confronter is concerned that the organization may be making a decision contrary to the desires of any of its members. A statement such as the following demonstrates the beginning of such an approach:

> I want to talk with you about the research project. Although I have previously said things to the contrary, I frankly don't think it will work, and I am very anxious about it. I suspect others may feel the same, but I don't know. Anyway, I am concerned that I may end up misleading you and that we may end up misleading one another, and if we aren't careful, we may continue to work on a project that none of us wants and that might even bankrupt us. That's why I need to know where the rest of you stand. I would appreciate any of your thoughts about the project. Do you think it can succeed?

What kinds of results can the confronter expect? I have found that the results can be divided into two categories: technical and existential. I have also found that for the person who initiates the confrontation, the existential experience takes precedence in the ultimate evaluation of the outcome of the action.

Technical Results. If the presence of the paradox has been correctly diagnosed, I have found that the solution to the technical problem may be almost absurdly quick and simple—something on the order of: "Do you mean that we have all been dragging along with a research project that none of us has thought would work? It's crazy. I can't believe we would do it, but we did. Let's figure out how we can cancel it and get to doing something productive."

The simplicity and rapidity of such a solution frequently don't seem possible to most of us, because we have been trained to believe that the solution to conflict requires a long, arduous process of debilitating problem solving.

Also, since existential risk is always present, it is possible that the diagnosis was incorrect, and the process of confrontation lifts to the level of public examination of real, substantive conflict, which may result in heated debates about technology, personalities, and/or administrative approaches. There is evidence that such debates, properly managed, can be the basis for creativity in organizational problem solving. There is also the possibility, however, that such debates cannot be managed and — substantiating the concept of existential risk — that the person who initiates the risk may get fired or ostracized. But that, again, leads to the necessity of evaluating the results of such confrontation at the existential level.

Existential Results. Evaluating the outcome of confrontation within an existential framework is quite different from evaluating it from a set of technical criteria. I have reached this conclusion simply by interviewing a variety of people who have chosen to confront the paradox and listening to their responses. In short, the psychological success and failure of Abilene Paradox confrontation apparently are divorced from what are traditionally accepted in organizations as criteria for success and failure.

For instance, some examples of success are described when people are asked, "What happened when you confronted the issue?" One person may answer: "I was told we had enough boat rockers in the organization, and I got fired. It hurt at first, but in retrospect it was the greatest day of my life. I've got another job and I'm delighted. I'm a free man." Another description of success might be: "I said I don't think the research project can succeed and the others looked shocked and quickly agreed. The upshot of the whole deal is that I got a promotion and am now known as a 'rising star.' It was the high point of my career."

Similarly, those who fail to confront the paradox describe failure in terms that are divorced from technical results. For example, one may report: "I didn't say anything, and we rocked along until the whole thing exploded and Joe got fired. There is still a lot of tension in the organization, and we are still in trouble, but I got a good performance review last time. I still feel lousy about the whole thing, though." From a different viewpoint, an individual may describe the feeling of failure in these words: "I knew I should have said something and I didn't. When the project failed, I was a convenient whipping boy. I got demoted. I still have a job, but my future here is definitely limited. In a way I deserve what I got, but it doesn't make it any easier to accept because of that."

Most important, the act of confrontation apparently provides intrinsic psychological satisfaction, regardless of the technological outcomes for those who attempt it. The real meaning of that existential experience, and its relevance to a wide variety of organizations, may lie, therefore, not in the scientific analysis of decision making but in an understanding of the plight of Sisyphus. That is something readers will have to decide for themselves.

The Abilene Paradox and the Myth of Sisyphus

As you may remember, Sisyphus was condemned by Pluto to a perpetuity of pushing a large stone to the top of a mountain, only to see it return to its original position when he released it. As Camus suggested in his revision of the myth, the task of Sisyphus was absurd and totally devoid of meaning. For most of us, though, the lives we lead—pushing papers or hubcaps—are no less absurd, and in many ways we probably spend about as much time "pushing rocks" in our organizations as Sisyphus did in his.

Camus also points out, though, that on occasion, as Sisyphus released his rock and watched it return to its resting place at the bottom of the hill, he was able to recognize the absurdity of his lot and, for brief periods of time, transcend it.

So it may be with confronting the Abilene Paradox. Confronting the absurd paradox of agreement may provide, through activity, what Sisyphus gained from his passive but conscious acceptance of his fate. Thus, through the process of active confrontation with reality, we may take respite from pushing our rocks on their endless journeys and, for brief moments, experience what C.P. Snow termed "the triumphs of life we make for ourselves"[10] within those absurdities we call organizations.

3

Organizations as Phrog Farms

A SHORT time ago, I received a telephone call from a friend who was employed as human resources director of a large corporation.

"Jerry, I've just been fired," he said.

"Fired? You mean you are out of a job completely?"

"Well, not completely," he replied. "I'm just no longer a director. In fact, my whole function has been wiped out. They have given me a make-work job in salary administration. It's a nothing job, though. I hate it. I was really interested in human resources. All I'm doing now is scut work and drawing a paycheck."

"Why were you fired, Hank?"

"I'm not really sure. I've never heard the reason directly. My boss's boss was the one who really did the firing. He told my boss to do it."

"Why did he tell your boss he wanted you fired?"

"My boss was vague about it. He just said his boss had said I wasn't powerful enough to do the job."

"What did your boss's boss say to you when you asked him about it?"

"I haven't talked with him."

"Why not?"

"That would be violating the chain of command. You don't do that around here."

"Why not?"

"You can get fired for that."

"But Hank," I said, "you have been fired."

"Oh!"

And then, perhaps because I had recently read my children the fable of *The Princess and the Frog*, [1] I said, "Hank, your boss's boss is correct. You aren't powerful enough to do the job. In fact, for all intents and purposes, he has turned you into a phrog. I can almost see you in a big phrog pond with your boss's boss sitting on a willow stump saying to himself, 'I think I'll turn ol' Hank into a phrog. And then he waves a magic wand, mutters some mystical-sounding incantation and concludes with, 'Hank, you are a phrog,' and suddenly you have web feet. Hank, you are now a phrog."

The silence at the other end of the line seemed interminable. Finally, a poignant, one-word reply echoed down the line: "Ribbit."

Phrog Farms

After talking with Hank at some length about his life in the phrog pond, I got to thinking that most formal organizations are, metaphorically speaking, phrog farms. By phrog farms, I mean that they turn a lot of good people into phrogs. In addition, if we accept the metaphor of organizations as phrog farms, we might conceptualize management improvement as the process of draining the swamp. Therefore, building upon that metaphor, I would like to suggest a number of hypotheses, make some generalizations, and conceptualize some issues of management within the framework of life in the swamp. The following statements are provided in no particular order of importance and in no conscious linear sequence:

1. All organizations have two essential purposes. One is to produce widgets, glops, and fillips. The other is to turn people into phrogs. In many organizations, the latter purpose takes precedence over the former. For example, in many organizations, it is more important to follow the chain of command than to behave sensibly.

2. Phrog is spelled with a *ph* because phrogs don't like to be known as frogs, and they try to hide their phroginess from themselves and others by transparent means. In short, once one has been transformed into a phrog, one likes to attempt to hide that fact. For one who has been a person, it's a great comedown to be a phrog.

3. Phrogs tend to live a solitary life in the swamp, or as one phrog said, "It's a lonely life on the lily pad." Phrogs compete with one another for insects, vie for the right to head the flicking order of the swamp, and are ultimately evaluated for what they do in their own mud flats. Furthermore, phrogs don't really get rewarded for how well they sing in the chorus. Given all that, is it any wonder that a common phrog maxim is, "You can't get involved with other phrogs in the swamp; someday you may have to appropriate their lily pads"?

4. Phrogs speak the language of Ribbit. It is a simple language in that it contains only one word, but it doesn't communicate very well. When all the phrogs in the swamp croak, "Ribbit," the swamp is noisy as hell, but not a lot of real information is ever exchanged. You see, accuracy of information is not very important in the swamp. In fact, any time a person enters the swamp, he or she is generally told that Ribbit is the only possible language of the swamp, despite the fact that phrogs don't learn much from one another when they use it. For that reason, people have a difficult time talking with phrogs. In fact, they seldom talk with phrogs at all.

5. Most phrogs spend more time flicking flies in the fog than draining the swamp. It seems that their behavior is circular. If they were to spend time draining the swamp, there would be no flies to flick—and no phrogs. For that reason, it's very important to phrogs to maintain the swamp as it is rather than to drain it.

6. In phrog farms, bullphrogs generally get to be phresident. In other words, the better a phrog can tolerate the loneliness of his lily pad, the more competent he becomes at speaking Ribbit, the more facile he becomes in flicking flies, the more skillful he becomes at appropriating others' lily pads, and the more adroit he becomes at maintaining the swamp, the more likely he is to become phresident.

7. Bullphrogs are greatly revered in the swamp. In fact, other phrogs assume that bullphrogs have magical powers because of their unusual abilities to turn people into phrogs. In one sense, such reverence may not be misplaced. Bullphrogs are apparently instrumental in the process of phrog production. It is strange, though, that we have devoted so little effort to understanding the role that humans play in permitting phrogs to attack them in the swamp.

8. The magic exercised by bullphrogs comes from humans' belief in it. The tyranny of bullphrogs stems not from the reality of bullphrogs' power, but from the human belief of the myth of "bullphrog power." Belief in bullphrog power prevents humans from having to take responsibility for the fog and mud and moss that make up the atmosphere of the swamp.

9. Bullphrogs—particularly phresidents—frequently feel very trapped in the swamp. Many of them are destroyed by it. They feel trapped because they *are* trapped. (Mr. Nixon was not an aberration.)

10. One of the peculiarities of the swamp is that the masses of swamp phrogs both worship and destroy bullphrogs for the very qualities of phroginess that resulted in their becoming phresident.

11. Darwinians say only the strongest go to the top of the phylogenetic scale. Phrogologists say only the weakest go to the top of the same scale. Both say only the fittest survive. One is incorrect.

12. Another peculiarity of the swamp is that cowphrogs seldom become phresident. Cowphrogs apparently don't have the capacity for loneliness, for speaking Ribbit, for fly flicking, and for swamp maintenance that bullphrogs have. If, by chance, they do develop that revered capacity, they become cowphrogs in bullphrogs' clothing—and their croaks deepen.

13. The process of producing phrogs is not sexual—it's magical—whereas the process of producing humans is sexual, great fun, and very real.

14. Management improvement programs generally consist of phrog kissing, which is magical, harmless, and platonic. Any activity designed to facilitate phrog kissing is cosmetic organizational development an example of ODD behavior—that is, *o*rganizational *d*evelopment, by *d*eception—or organizational improvement as practiced by phrogs. Activities such as phrog style assessment, phrog chorus-building, and inter-lily-pad conflict resolution, in the absence of swamp drainage and area reclamation, are examples of phrog kissing by ODD managers.

15. Phrog kissing is a seductive activity. Frederick Herzberg claims that being seduced is ultimately less satisfying than being raped, because when we are seduced, we are, in fact, part of our own down-

fall.[2] Stated differently, in our context, managerial reformers are frequently seduced into phrog kissing, an activity that seldom leads to lovemaking but frequently adds to the warts on the kisser's face.

16. Many organization members belong to phrognarian networks and swamp maintenance associations. The purpose of such networks and associations is to meet and exchange information regarding the nature of the fog in each member's respective swamp. Since the language of Ribbit is employed, such exchanges seldom allow anyone to differentiate one swamp from another. Phrogs seem to get reassurance from noting the similarity among their swamps. Or, as one bullphrog put it, "Misery loves company and miserable phrogs love miserable companies."

17. Occasionally, during meetings of Phrognarians, a phrog pharts in the fog. When that happens, the phrog loses some of his or her phroginess and, therefore, represents a great threat to the balance of the swamp. Phrog pharts are seldom sanctioned by Phrognarians. They are too real. They put holes in the fog and ultimately threaten the atmosphere of magic required to maintain the swamp.

18. There is a myth among phrogs that kissing another phrog turns that phrog into a prince. I think it should be noted that, in general, kissing a phrog only produces skin irritations. For those who decide to kiss anyway, I think they should also realize that, in all that fog, it is very difficult to determine which way a phrog is facing.

19. Phrogs frequently try to set traps for one another. Phrog traps have a peculiar quality, however, in that they catch only the phrogs who set them. In other words, if you have to set a phrog trap, there is no need to do so—you are already in it.

20. So that the technology of setting phrog traps is not lost to future generations, phrogfessors of marsh management are hired by schools of swamp maintenance to research and teach. The work of such phrogfessors is governed by the underlying credo that is frequently displayed on their respective lily pads: "If the tadpole hasn't learned, the phrogfessor hasn't taught."

The underlying rationale of that credo is rather peculiar when we subject it to close scrutiny. It clearly implies that the basic responsibility for the tadpole's learning belongs to the phrogfessor. Consequently, if the tadpole does a lousy job, the phrogfessor is at fault. Likewise, following the same logic rigorously, if the tadpole does competent work, the phrogfessor must also get the credit. For all intents and purposes, then, the tadpole doesn't exist, except as some sort of inanimate, passive receptacle for the phrogfessor's competence or incompetence.

Since such a teaching attitude implies that students have no animate existence, is it any wonder that swamp administration graduates seem to fit so well into the lonely parallelism of the swamp? Is it also any wonder that when someone accepts responsibility for another's learning, that person ceases to be an educator and becomes a phrogfessor, whose primary job is to prepare tadpoles for life in the swamp?

21. People frequently become phrogs in other kinds of organizations by the same process. After all, a common swamp saying is, "You can delegate authority but you can't delegate responsibility." Translation: "You are responsible for your subordinates' performances. If your subordinates perform competently, it is because of you. If they perform incompetently, it is because of you, too. Like students, subordinates exist only as extensions of you. They are objects you must manipulate in the best interests of the swamp."

If phrogs don't feel that they are responsible for the performance of their subordinates, then why do so many of them go to training programs designed to help them alter their phrogging styles? As I see it, they do it because they believe that they are responsible for their subordinates' performances and that their style (as opposed to their essence) has something to do with how effectively their subordinates perform.

22. All of us are phrogs at one time or another. We all have the potential to develop webbing between our toes. We all have experienced the terror of the trap—and accepting responsibility for others' actions is the bait with which phrog traps are set.

23. Many bullphrogs can't laugh at the absurdity of their lives in the swamp. Such phrogs tend to become steerphrogs, which are very poignant creatures. Bullphrogs frequently die laughing, but I have never seen a steerphrog laugh. They just croak.

24. The seat of the U.S. government is located in Washington, D.C., in a swampy area of the city known affectionately to some as

"Foggy Bottom." For many, it is also the locus of the bureaucratic mess. Perhaps it should be renamed, Phroggy Bottom.

25. Alfred Marrow's *Making Waves in Foggy Bottom* is about an effort to clean up the bureaucratic mess in the U.S. Department of State.[3] In essence, the book is about the failure of that effort. If you read it, you might come to realize that making waves—in any organization—is a very different process from draining the swamp.

26. The size of the swamp is growing; the world may ultimately be inhabited entirely by phrogs. Air pollution is not really as great a threat to future generations as phrog pollution. The swamp is ultimately evil. As Hannah Arendt described the situation, phrog farms, despite their benign appearance, tend to develop bullphrogs with an enormous capacity for evil.[4] (Adolph Eichmann was not an aberration, either.)

27. The job of most swamp managers is to maintain and enhance the swamp, not to drain it. As Winston Phroghill said, "I was not made marsh minister to preside over the draining of the swamp."

28. The purpose of swamp consultants—in the eyes of swamp managers—is to help the swamp operate effectively, not to drain it.

29. Most management improvement literature is designed to facilitate swamp management, not area reclamation. Most managers are phrog farmers, and most management consultants and phrogfessors of marsh management are phrog farmers' helpers. The relationship is symbiotic.

30. Most phrog farmers and their helpers are aware that they are mired in the swamp. Most have about all the consciousness they can bear. May God have mercy on their souls.

31. God does have mercy on their souls. Otherwise, God would be the greatest phrog farmer of them all.

Alternatives to Life on the Phrog Farm

It's a lonely life on the lily pad. What are some possible alternatives to life in the swamp? Phrogs can't survive outside the swamp, but human managers *might* escape the swamp by the following means:

1. Paying employees as pairs, teams, or organizations, rather than as individuals: When two or more individuals get paid for working

together, it is amazing how much interest they take in helping one another succeed.

2. Developing non-zero-sum climates when it comes to promotions, layoffs, salaries, performance appraisals, and grades: People with zero-sum attitudes believe that the outcome of any interpersonal encounter is zero; that is, "If you get a payoff of plus one, I must get a payoff of minus one, and the outcome is zero" or "If you win, I must lose." People with non-zero-sum attitudes believe that the outcome of any human encounter can be other than zero; that is, we can both win and, if we do, under certain conditions, it is not one plus one equals two but rather, with synergy, three. For example, during bad times, phrogs lay others off according to seniority. People *don't* lay one another off; they all take proportionate pay cuts and thus learn that they can rely on one another during both good and bad times.

3. Leaving the environment when they lose interest in it: For example, regarding vesting of pension rights, people don't wear vests—phrogs do.

4. Accepting personal responsibility for their own activities in the organization: For instance, phrogs demand that bullphrogs take full responsibility for the swamp. People will not permit others to take over their responsibilities for the habitat and its operation.

5. Trusting one another in a wide variety of situations: Phrogs distrust just about everybody. They put in time clocks, which say, "We don't trust you to do an honest day's work, so prove that you did." They demand doctors' certificates when someone calls in ill. They have private offices so that others' access to them is limited and so that their conversations and work with other phrogs can't be observed and overheard. They demand close verification of expense accounts because "everyone knows those slick swamp salesmen would rob the marsh blind if a bullphrog doesn't keep tabs on them." They keep cover-your-ass (CYA) files to protect themselves from other phrogs' poison kisses. By contrast, people have very few rules and procedures that question the honesty of others. In fact, they assume that other people can be trusted and live with the reality that in a few cases, such trust will be violated.

6. Treating others subjectively, not objectively: R.D. Laing has

pointed out that one way to make others mentally ill is to treat them as depersonalized objects or things, (that is, objectively) rather than as "personalized" subjects (that is, subjectively).[5] Bullphrogs try to treat others objectively. They try to gauge the performance of others objectively, and they try to "keep their feelings out of the situation." However, when you treat another objectively (that is, as an object), you should know that the price of being objective — eliminating your feelings from the situation — is that you become an object yourself, since you have denied the very essence of your own humanness. Thus are bullphrogs born. Humans don't treat one another as objects. They try, instead, to build a work environment in which human subjectivity is accepted as an integral part of the habitat's problem-solving process.

After reading my ideas concerning possible approaches to swamp drainage and area reclamation, some of you may say, "Your ideas are too vague, idealistic, and impractical. They certainly are not of much use to those of us who have spent our lives in the swamp." I hope you don't feel that way, but if you do, about all I can say is that I trust your judgment. But I tried, as only a phrogfessor could.

Ribbit.

4

Management and the Myth of Abraham: or, Go Plant a Cabbage on God's Behalf

B ROTHERS and sisters of the Church of Perpetual Bureaucracy, in today's sermon I will explore how several commonplace, yet corrosive, management practices have gained legitimacy because they reflect an accepted interpretation of a revered religious belief. Specifically, I will explore how we managers use some of the thought patterns attributed to our ancient bureaucratic biblical brother, Abraham, to justify deceiving other members of our organizations, abusing innocent subordinates in the service of narcissistic self-interest, and releasing ourselves from accepting moral responsibility for perpetrating such abuse. Then I will describe how we blame our superiors for whatever problems our lack of integrity may create for ourselves and others. Finally, I will suggest how the staff of the Great CEO in the Sky might rewrite the story of Abraham in order to further organizational goals.

Please open your Bibles to the twenty-second chapter of Genesis and read silently with me as I recount that great tale of the failure of religious and organizational faith, the story of God, Abraham, Isaac, Sarah, and Associates. I read from *The Living Bible (Paraphrased)* beginning with verse one and proceeding through verse eighteen.[1]

The Story of Abraham and Isaac

Verse one: "Later on God tested Abraham's faith and obedience." Apparently, loyalty tests didn't begin with the medieval rulers who spread false rumors of their own impending deaths in order to ascertain which servants would be loyal during times of crisis. Nor did the practice end with Senator McCarthy's hearings or President Reagan's penchant for lie detector tests. Authority figures always distrust their subordinates; and God, according to the author (or authors) of Genesis, was no different from anyone else.

"Abraham!" God called.

"Yes, Lord!" Abraham replied.

"Take with you your only son—yes, Isaac whom you love so much—and go to the land of Moriah and sacrifice him there as a burnt offering upon one of the mountains which I'll point out to you."

Now, brother and sister bureaucrats, as you know, the Great CEO in the Sky was not asking for what one might call a "small sacrifice." Abraham was 100 years old when he had the uplifting experience of successfully impregnating his wife, Sarah, who at age 90 was herself no spring chicken. In addition, the birth of the child gave Abraham and Sarah much joy—so much joy that they named him Isaac, which meant "laughter." I suppose you could say that the Great CEO in the Sky was asking him to kill laughter. Perhaps that's why many organizations are so devoid of humor. (For instance, have you ever noticed that the annual reports of formal organizations are seldom as funny as the way those organizations actually operate?) The desire to kill laughter may be the reason why employment advertisements often seek "no-nonsense" managers. Can you think of less interesting or more incompetent managers than those who pride themselves on not engaging in nonsense?

Anyway, "The next morning Abraham got up early, chopped wood, saddled his donkey, took with him his son, Isaac, and two young men who were his servants and started off to the place where God had told him to go.[a] On the third day of the journey Abraham saw the place in the distance."

Now, brothers and sisters, I ask you, does the whole situation make

---

[a] To the best of my knowledge, the two young men were members of the first personnel department, and their job was to "grease the skids" for the RIF (reduction in force). Today they would probably be called outplacement specialists or downsizing facilitators, and they would report to the director of human resources.

much sense? Did Abraham say, "Can you explain why you want me to kill my boy?" or did he plead, "Kill me instead," or did he ask, "How about letting me have some time to talk it over with Sarah? She might have some feelings about this, too, you know." As you are probably aware, the answer is no. Thus, Abraham's unquestioning obedience to his superior established and gave holy sanction to the age-old bureaucratic dictum: "It is more important to obey authority than to behave sensibly." Adolph Eichmann and many of the rest of us are thereby bureaucratic kinfolk to God's executive vice-president, Abraham.

But the story of organizational intrigue does not end there. "Stay here with the donkey," Abraham told the young men, "and the lad and I will travel yonder and worship and then come right back."

Significantly, in this story we can see the genesis of several commonplace bureaucratic thought patterns. Abraham relegated the two young men—the representatives of the personnel department—to a peripheral role, perhaps because the grisly task involved a major moral issue. Possibly, he feared that the young men would get in the way by offering moral or ethical alternatives. Worse yet, they might stage a rebellion. Regardless of his motivation, it is clear that he had no need to worry. Those who would consent to stand around passively holding a jackass during a time of moral crisis pose no threat. They do, however, serve as long-term role models for others who might follow.

Returning to the story: "Abraham placed the wood for the burnt offering upon Isaac's shoulders, while he himself carried the knife and the flint for striking a fire. So the two of them went on together." It is important to note that Isaac carried his own "walking papers," unaware of his role in the impending restructuring of the organization and the coincident reallocation of key personnel. In other words, he didn't know he was about to get fired, both literally and figuratively.

The story becomes even more complex in verse seven, when Isaac asked, "Father, we have the wood and the flint to make the fire, but where is the lamb for the sacrifice?"

Abraham answered with a lie—a clear, unequivocal act of deception—when he said, "God will see to it, my son," knowing full well that God had already made the decision about who would be the sacrificial lamb. His answer is representative of the standard, bureaucratic reassurances a superior might mendaciously give to a subordinate who is worried about an RIF.

Abraham evidently had learned an early version of Boren's law, which states: "When in doubt, mumble. When cornered, obfuscate."[2] An updated version of Abraham's reply to Isaac might be: "What we must do is consider your question in the light of the pros and cons, given the exigencies of the situation, to ensure that the best interests of all are met within the framework of the long-term developmental plan, the financial issues so central to the problem and its solution, and the political climate under which a wide variety of conflicting crosscurrents operate." Later on, Abraham probably said to his associates, "I didn't actually lie to him. I just didn't tell him everything I knew."

Faced with such babble, Isaac capitulated. Or, in the metaphor of a much later minor prophet who wrote about organizations as phrog farms (see chapter 3), Isaac—following the model set by both his father and the personnel specialists—became a toady and kissed the phrog. Apparently, in the fog, Isaac was unable to see which direction the phrog was facing and was also unaware that phrog kissing is a seductive activity that seldom leads to lovemaking but generally adds to the warts on the kisser's face.

Regardless of Isaac's perceptiveness or lack thereof, the Scripture says: "They went on. When they arrived at the place where God had told Abraham to go, he built an altar and placed the wood in order, ready for the fire,[b] and then tied Isaac and laid him on the altar over

---

[b]I am always impressed with the origin of the English use of the expression *fire* to mean "terminate employment." According to Mathew's *Dictionary of Americanisms* (Chicago: University of Chicago Press, 1951, p. 611), that idiom was first used in 1871 and meant "to eject or throw (a person) bodily from a place, to put out by forcible means." Another explanation, which I have not been able to verify by scholarly means, came from a guide aboard the colonial era warship, the *Constellation*. The guide contended that the word originated in the early U.S. Navy when sailors who were discipline problems were spread-eagled over the end of cannons and "fired." Whether you prefer a scholarly or fanciful explanation, it is clear that being fired is not associated in our minds with acts of compassionate love.

the wood. And Abraham took the knife and lifted it up to plunge it into his son, to slay him."

Then, brothers and sisters, the story takes a very interesting twist, because it says, "At that moment the Angel of God shouted to him from heaven, 'Abraham! Abraham!' "

And Abraham, ever sensitive to the wishes of his boss, answered, "Yes, Lord."

"Lay down the knife; don't hurt the lad in any way," the Angel said, "for I know that God is first in your life—you have not withheld even your beloved son from me."

Now, to begin with, I'm always intrigued that the message to stop the sacrifice came from the Angel of God, not from God himself. In fact, it seems as if any time a boss makes a stupid mistake, he sends his administrative assistant to try to rectify it. Anyway, Abraham obeyed the directive relayed by God's administrative assistant, noticed a ram caught in a nearby bush, and sacrificed it instead. Most organizations find scapegoats when they make dumb errors. Sometimes it is Oliver North. Other times it is a ram.

Then, if you continue to read, you will find that the Great CEO in the Sky used his administrative assistant to relay another message. This missive announced a bonus for his loyal subordinate: "Because you have obeyed me and have not withheld even your beloved son from me, I will bless you with incredible blessings and multiply your descendants into thousands and millions . . . all because you have obeyed me."

Now, I ask you, what could we call Abraham's willingness to kill his beloved son without a reason other than complying with his boss's desire that he pass a loyalty test? Well, Soren Kierkegaard, the protestant existential theologian, in an essay entitled "Fear and Trembling," calls Abraham's willingness to obey God's command an extraordinary, virtually incomprehensible act of religious faith.[3] Kierkegaard and many other theologians seem to agree that Abraham's unquestioning obedience to God's unreasonable command is a prototypical act of religious faith, one that offers a model for only the most disciplined believers, regardless of the religious tradition they espouse.

The Neighbor's Sacrifice

"But," you may ask, "how does the story of Abraham's act of religious faith have anything to do with contemporary management and organization?" Well, brothers and sisters, if you do have such a question, I will try to answer it.

You, sir—you near the aisle—will you get me a glass of water? Now you—you, there, in the front pew—do you have a neighbor? Ah, good. What's the neighbor's name? Abe? What a coincidence! And does Abe have a son? He does? What's the son's name? Ah, Ike. That's a good name. Well, suppose you go home tonight and your neighbor comes through the gate in the back fence and says, "I just heard a voice calling to me from the trees in the backyard. It's God talking, for sure. He wants me to kill my only beloved son, Ike, and roast him on the barbecue pit as a way of proving my loyalty to him.ᶜ I need to borrow a knife with a serrated edge so I can make a quick, clean cut; and I also need to borrow some extra firewood. Ours is wet and doesn't burn easily. I'll send Ike over to pick it up. If he asks why I want firewood in the middle of a summer heat wave, just say, 'God only knows.' I'm going to send a couple of young men over to keep him occupied while I repair the barbecue pit and build the fire. I need to work fast because I want to get it done before Edna returns home. She tends to get agitated when I do things like this."

Now, what would you do in a situation like that? Yes, I agree with the lady in the left balcony, who shouted, "Call the police! Have him put in protective custody or sent to the funny farm!" Right. Because he is crazy, nuts, bonkers, and, ultimately, certifiably insane. Oh, amen, sister, amen.

But, dearly beloved, let's not permit the story to end there. Once you get Abe tranquilized, transported, incarcerated, and certified as mentally ill, you go home, go to bed, wake up the next morning, and go to your office.

ᶜBefore you dismiss my analogy as totally absurd, remember that the "Son of Sam" killer, David Berkowitz—a young man who in 1976 murdered six people in the New York City area—contended that he was instructed to do so by demons who spoke through the medium of a dog named Sam. See David Abrahamsen, *Confessions of Son of Sam* (New York: Columbia University Press, 1985).

Sacrifice at Work

Upon arrival, you are greeted by your boss—the organization's president, who says, "I'm going to put you to the test. I want you to fire fifty people. If we do it now, the bottom line for the fiscal quarter will look a lot better."

Let's assume that you are a tiny bit more assertive than our brother Abraham, and you say, "But sir, why? They haven't done anything wrong. They have worked hard, have done their jobs well, and have been faithful, hard-working employees."

To that your boss replies, "Be a loyal team player and do it because I told you so. And besides, if you do it competently, in a way that nobody gets too upset, no grievances are filed by the union, and the troops don't get restless and pull a wildcat strike on us, I will bless you, your division will multiply, you will get a 10 percent increase in salary, and I will name you executive vice-president."

After that explanation, what do most of us do? Right, as the lady in the choir said, we respond to the boss with: "Give me the list of those you want to get rid of" or, metaphorically, "Where do I collect the firewood?"

The Theology of Abraham at Work

What is the essential meaning of the foregoing three parables for those of us who, knowingly or unknowingly, adhere to the catechism of contemporary organizations?

Clearly, Abraham's willingness to kill his only son solely on God's behest is frequently termed an act of religious faith. I also think Abe's willingness to kill his son Ike would generally be called an act of insanity. But I believe it equally likely that your willingness to fire fifty employees for the purpose of "making the quarter look good" would be called an act of hardnosed managerial skill and would be an example of an action many managers believe is required to make organizations function effectively. But I ask you, what are the differences in the essential thought processes and underlying value systems of

Abraham, Abe, and those of us who would take such action in our managerial and organizational roles?

It seems to me that there is no difference. Each thought pattern reflects the belief that it is more important to obey authority than to think on our own. Each reflects the belief that lying and deception are legitimate forms of managerial behavior in organizational settings. Each reflects the protagonist's conviction that he or she is not responsible for his or her own actions. Rather, God (or some other authority figure) is responsible. In more contemporary terms, God can delegate authority, but he can't delegate responsibility. In that sense, comedian Flip Wilson, who became famous for saying, "The Devil made me do it"; the banal Nazi automaton Adolph Eichmann, who achieved a dubious immortality by contending, "I was only following orders"; and that paragon of religious faith, Abraham, who achieved prototypical religious status by demonstrating his willingness to kill his only begotten son, are bureaucratic brothers. Furthermore, to the extent that we demonstrate, through mimicking their actions, our implicit approval of their patterns of thought and the values that support them, we have become a part of their organizational family.

The story of Abraham, in my opinion, tells us little more about the essence of God than the ritual, laudatory press release tells stockholders about the essence of the CEO of Amalgamated, Incorporated. Rather, as the prophet Carl Jung tells us in "Answers to Job" and "Christ, a Symbol of the Self,"[4] our conception of God—the ultimate authority figure—is frequently clouded by our unconscious desire to release ourselves from accepting the responsibility for our actions toward one another and, in a more important sense, as Erich Fromm contended in *Escape from Freedom*,[5] to avoid the anxiety of being accountable for the choices we make as we go about our daily lives in all kinds of organizations. In other words, the story of Abraham and Isaac, which probably was concocted by an ancient image consultant, tells us nothing about God but does tell us a great deal about our desire to be released emotionally from accountability for hatred and consequent inhumanity toward our children, our families, our friends, our colleagues, and our bosses. As a result, so long as we can blame God, the devil, our parents, or the CEO—and, following the course set by Abraham, call our cop-out an act of faith rather than murder—we can always plead the Eichmann "defense" and receive the approbation that the custodial representatives of the secular gods offer for it.[d]

Lest you think that I exaggerate how much managers abdicate responsibility for inhumane decisions, I point to the reaction to a "sermon" I preached to managers some time ago. My "congregation" generally was from the personnel or the managerial priesthood of a variety of Churches of the Bureaucracy. One of the priests, in obedience to the commands from the god he worshipped, had recently sacrificed approximately fifty Isaacs from his organization in an effort to make the financial quarter look good. In great fury, he responded to my homily with a scathing denunciation of my thesis that firing Isaac, in the context of obedience to a capricious god, is an act of evil. Rather, he argued, firing faithful, competent, hard-working employees for the basic purpose of improving the short-term financial performance of the company would provide for their spiritual growth. (I think he specifically called the RIF a "personal growth experience" for the sacrificial lambs.) He argued that the slaughter would be growthful for the employees, because (1) it would teach them not to rely on any one employer or to put their trust in any one organization; (2) it would force them to learn new skills, which might be marketable elsewhere; (3) it would bring families together by forcing them to work together in order to survive; (4) it would teach them the ultimate truth that life is unfair; and (5) it might even drive them into the loving arms of the formal church in an effort to cope with the pain and suffering they would probably experience. In short, he concluded: "Firing others in such a way is ultimately a religious act, and it is for their own spiritual growth that it is done."

---

[d]It is interesting that, in *Fear and Trembling,* Kierkegaard very briefly considered the possibility that Abraham was abdicating his moral responsibility. However, Kierkegaard quickly rejected that notion—virtually without serious consideration—as if the thought or possibility was too overwhelming to bear. And some—for instance, Lowrie—wonder why the "melancholy Dane," unable to consider his own destructive impulses, suffered from chronic depression; see Walter Lowrie, *A Short Life of Kierkegaard* (Princeton, N.J.: Princeton University Press, 1970).

He received a standing ovation. May God have mercy on his soul. (God does have mercy on his soul; otherwise, God would be the greatest phrog farmer of them all.)

In an effort to keep you and me from joining Kierkegaard in his melancholy depression, let me say that I believe that there is hope. We need not be forever trapped by the story of Abraham and Isaac. We can write our own new story. God has given us the potential to reflect both his majestic anger and his unfathomable grace. Once that new story of Abraham and Isaac is written, it may provide us with moral, ethical, and spiritual guidelines for managing organizations in a manner consistent with God's essence, which is our own, assuming that we believe God made us in his image.

Of course, we would want the new story to portray respect for authority and realism, while it encourages us to be both responsible and accountable for our own actions. We also would want the new parable to be written so as to enhance the possibility that the organizations we build not only survive but flourish. Here's how the "New Myth of Abraham and Isaac" might go:

Later on, God tested Abraham's faith and obedience.

"Abraham!" God called.

"Yes, Lord?" Abraham replied.

"Take with you your only son—yes, Isaac, whom you love so much—and go to the land of Moriah and sacrifice him there as a burnt offering upon one of the mountains, which I'll point out to you!"

"God!"

"Yes, Abraham, my beloved servant."

"You must be kidding."

"Of course I'm not kidding, Abraham. Would I kid you on something like this?"

"Would you please excuse me a moment, Lord? I need to make a phone call."

And Abraham went to his inner office and called Sarah, his wife.

When Sarah answered, Abraham said, "Go and hide Isaac with some of the neighbors. I think God has been drinking again. He's making noises about wanting me to fire Isaac, plus the usual stuff about the need to make sacrifices and being a loyal team player. I think he's just tired, but you never know. And whatever you do, don't take calls from his administrative assistant. I'm going to try my best to talk him out of it, and I don't stand much of a chance of doing it if I have to work through one of his toadies."

The next hour, Abraham returned to the office and talked with God. And God asked, "Abraham, if you love Me and have faith in Me, you will kill Isaac, and roast him on your backyard barbecue pit as I have instructed you."

Abraham replied, "If you want Isaac killed, you will have to do it yourself. I love him dearly, and I know I don't have the power to stop you if you really want to kill him. But I don't think you will. I don't think you are that unfair. I love you, too, but not enough to do something crazy."

"Do you have faith in Me, Abraham?"

"I have faith enough to argue with you, but not enough faith to deny the wisdom and integrity you have given me."

"Abraham, my son, you are a pisser."

"I'll never be able to hit as high on the wall as you, God."

"Abraham, it has been a hard day. Famine in India, war in Afghanistan, the Pope has been shot, and a Californian is in the White House."

"It must be an awful burden to try to deal with all of that alone. Is there any way I can help out?"

And God said, "Yes."

And Abraham, bowing before God's majesty, said, "What?"

God replied, "Take your only beloved son, Isaac, and your wife, Sarah, and a few close friends and go plant a cabbage on a mountain in Moriah, which I will point out to you."[e]

"A cabbage, Lord?" said Abraham, again suspicious that God was in his cups.

"Yes. If all you do is plant a cabbage and do it well, it will make that part of the world a better place." And Abraham did as God requested.

Upon Abraham's return from Moriah, God said, "I, the Lord, have sworn by Myself that because you have disobeyed Me and have not followed my commands and yet have planted a cabbage on My behalf, I will bless you with incredible blessings and multiply your descendants into countless thousands and millions, like the stars above you in

---

[e]According to I.B. Myers, in her book *Gifts Differing* (Palo Alto, Calif.: Consulting Psychologists Press, 1980, p. 611), Jung made a similar suggestion.

the sky and like the sands along the seashore. These descendants of yours will conquer their enemies and be a blessing to all the nations of the earth, . . . for they will be blessed with abundant cabbages."

Brothers and sisters of the Church of Perpetual Bureaucracy, rather than railing against the deception, the blind obedience to authority and a capricious God who demands that we violate the truth in ourselves and him—in short, rather than cursing the darkness of our self-generated bureaucratic heritage and calling it faith—I suggest that each of us go plant a cabbage on God's behalf.

Amen.

5

Captain Asoh and the Concept of Grace

W HEN we make it difficult for organization members to acknowledge their mistakes and have them forgiven, we have designed organizations that reduce risk taking, encourage lying, foment distrust, and, as a consequence, decrease productivity.

For example, in the U.S. military, officers are subjected to the "doctrine of zero defects."[1] Officially, the doctrine is designed to encourage double-checking of the operation and maintenance of inherently dangerous and easily damaged mechanical systems. The justification for a zero-defects policy in such activities as aircraft maintenance and nuclear weapons handling is obvious. But the doctrine has been extended—at least informally—to nonmechanical systems, so that officers who make significant mistakes of any sort destroy their long-term careers, because once mistakes are documented and become part of personnel files, they are virtually impossible to "erase." Therefore, any major mechanical, managerial, or social mistake becomes a constant impediment to promotion—particularly promotion to the higher ranks, where the competition is most intense.

Adherents of several religious traditions define *grace* as forgiveness raised to the highest level in the form of unmerited favor. Evidently, grace is not an integral part of the military's personnel system.

Because military personnel know that their careers depend upon error-free records and because they are aware that mistakes are unlikely to be forgiven, many officers "shade the truth" in their reports to superiors, learn to distrust one another, and become cautious and noninnovative in their approach to problem solving. The result is disastrous. As one officer said, "You show me an officer who hasn't made a mistake in a year or two and I'll show you a man who has been afraid to try anything."[2]

I would expand his comment: "You show me a manager, subordinate, teacher, preacher, student, parent, child, politician, or anyone else who hasn't made a mistake in a year or two, and I'll show you someone who has been afraid to try anything of significance."

The reluctance to forgive and the consequences of such reluctance are not unique to the military. Should you doubt the validity of that assertion, try to get an F expunged from your university transcript for the semester you lost interest in school because of a broken romance; or try to get a poor performance appraisal—written by an incompetent supervisor—removed from your company's personnel records; or try to get the record of your arrest for a minor teenage indiscretion removed from your police file after twenty years of exemplary conduct as an adult.

In fact, cautious inactivity occurs in virtually all formal organizations, because we generally have no processes, procedures, or policies for granting forgiveness. This is particularly unfortunate, since the ancillary effects of grace are risk taking, innovation, reality testing, and community building. It is interesting that although forgiveness is absent from the formal organizations in which we spend a fair proportion of our lives, it tends to be integral to the religious traditions that govern us outside those organizations. I think one can say, without doubt, that forgiveness—"the willingness to give up resentment . . . or claim to requital" (Webster's Seventh New Collegiate Dictionary, 1969)—is one of the cornerstones of the Judeo-Christian religious tradition. It perhaps receives its highest form of expression in the concept of grace. Grace, in turn, is defined by Merriam-Webster as "unmerited divine assistance given man for his regeneration or sanctification." And Paul Achtemeir calls grace "that which brings delight, joy, happiness . . . the good fortune, kindness and power bestowed by the gods upon divine men, moving them to miraculous deeds."[3]

The need for organizational policies, procedures, and processes that facilitate forgiveness and grace became vividly apparent to me a couple of years ago when a neighbor, Ed, who is a commercial airline pilot, made a mistake when recording his work schedule in his calendar. As a result, he failed to show up to fly his plane on its journey from the East Coast of the United States to Bermuda. It seems that neither the ninety-odd snow-crusted passengers—primed for their February vacations in the sun—nor the airline's managers, who had to cope with the ensuing customer complaints, were exactly overwhelmed with gratitude for Ed's forgetfulness. In short, when a pilot doesn't appear in the cockpit at the appointed hour, it is considered "poor form" by almost everybody. Clearly worried, Ed told me about the event and about a rather ominous-sounding internal investigation that would take place the next day at company headquarters.

"Are you in serious trouble?" I asked.

"Very serious trouble," he replied. "I could get fined, reduced in rank, suspended, dropped in seniority, or fired. They can do damn near anything to me, and about all I can do is take it."

"My God, Ed, that sounds awful. What are you going to do?"

"I'm going to invoke the Asoh defense," said he, apparently assuming that I would know exactly what his intentions were. Since I didn't, I asked for a more comprehensive explanation, and that is how I learned the story of Captain Asoh and the concept of grace.

The Captain Asoh Story

It seems that Captain Asoh—Captain Kohei Asoh to be exact—was the Japan Air Lines pilot who, on November 22, 1968, landed his DC-8 jet—with ninety-six passengers and eleven crew members aboard—two and a half miles out in San Francisco Bay but in nearly exact compass line with the runway. According to Ed's version of the affair, Captain Asoh landed the plane so gently that many of the passengers were unaware that they were in the water until someone pointed out a sailboat on the port bow. Ed further contends that Captain Asoh landed it so expertly that no one was injured, no one was bruised, and no one even got wet feet as the passengers were rowed in inflatable life rafts to the nearest land. Even the airplane suffered only minor structural damage, and it was salvaged before the ravages of irreversible salt water corrosion set in. Regardless of how competently he did it, though, the fact that Captain Asoh, a veteran pilot with approximately 10,000 hours of flying time, landed his plane two and a half miles out in the bay irritated a large number of people.

Shortly afterward, the National Transportation Safety Board (NTSB) held a preliminary hearing to set the ground rules for what they and others assumed would be a minimum of six months of bitter, recriminatory testimony to determine who was at fault, who was to blame for the debacle. According to the story told by pilots, lawyers were leasing suites at nearby hotels in preparation for the "vicious battle" to follow. Newspaper reporters and TV crews were assembling en masse to cover the public hearings. Representatives of foreign governments were rushing to San Francisco to ensure that the interests of their citizens would be protected.

In short, the whole thought process and consequent investigative procedures were predicated on the assumption that the proceedings inevitably would be adversarial and that the task of finding the culprit (or culprits) responsible for the accident would be, at best, difficult or, at worst, nearly impossible.

Captain Asoh, however, was of a different mentality. He apparently failed to realize that most of us live by Ogden Nash's credo: "Never apologize; never explain." Captain Asoh seemed unaffected by the common assumption that forgiveness by formal organizations is unlikely and that any admission of fault, culpability, or wrongdoing is the preamble to personal calamity. Alternatively, Asoh may have assumed that everyone's interests in an organization are best served by actions that open up the possibility of graceful forgiveness and consequent reconciliation.[a]

Captain Asoh was the hearing's first witness. The eyes and ears of the world were focused upon him – including those of private citizens,

---

[a]Japanese organizations have what I call ceremonies of *wa* ("harmony") to facilitate such reconciliation. In these "ceremonies," individuals who have made serious mistakes apologize for their actions and other members of the organization accept their apologies, restoring harmony by wiping the slate clean. See R. Whiting, "You've Gotta Have 'Wa.'" *Sports Illustrated*, 24 September 1979, 59–62+, for an example of that approach to improving organizational climate.

angry passengers, representatives of pilots' associations, lawyers, newspaper reporters, and representatives of a variety of governments—and all persons present leaned forward and braced for the conflagration that it seemed would inevitably follow. Asoh took the stand, and—as the story goes—the investigator in charge opened the hearing with the penetrating question: "Captain Asoh, in your own words, can you tell us how you managed to land that DC-8 Stretch Jet two and a half miles out in San Francisco Bay in perfect compass line with the runway?"

Asoh's reply was, "As you Americans say, Asoh fuck up!"

According to the story recounted by my pilot friend, with those words, the hearing was concluded. All had been said that could be said, and nothing more of consequence could be added. Only "details" remained to be clarified.

Since my neighbor first told me the story, I have scoured newspapers, talked with three of the persons who investigated the accident for the National Transportation Safety Board, spoken with a representative of Japan Air Lines, and read the *Aircraft Accident Report*.[4] One of the NTSB investigators that I interviewed said, "Although I didn't hear him say those exact words, one might argue they in effect capture the essence of what he said," and another NTSB investigator indicated that profanity is frequently censored from the final NTSB public reports, but I found no direct evidence that the captain had described his role in the accident so colorfully.

Without such definitive verification, I have concluded that the story's memorable conclusion is clearly apocryphal. However, I am equally certain that the story itself expresses a broader reality that many of us wish and know to be true. For instance, Rod MacLeish, in a *Washington Star* article entitled "The Fine Art of Apology," conjectured that Richard Nixon probably would have completed his term as president if he had possessed the combination of integrity and common sense required to offer contrition that essentially would have amounted to invoking the Asoh defense.[5] Had Mr. Nixon actually invoked the Asoh defense, I doubt that any of us would ever have forgotten the press conference in which he did it.

I have observed that airline pilots throughout the world are familiar with the story of Captain Asoh and are willing—even eager—to recount his exploit at the drop of landing gear. A short time ago, I happened to sit next to an off-duty airline captain who was flying across the country to attend his daughter's wedding. Upon learning of his occupation, I inquired, rather tentatively, "I'm a university professor doing some research on the possible role forgiveness plays in organizations, and I wonder, have you ever heard of someone in your profession by the name of Captain Asoh?" In a loud voice, audible throughout much of the airplane, he shouted, "Asoh fuck up!" Consequently, throughout the remainder of the flight, we were treated as semiperverts by most of our fellow passengers, who were on their way to a national convention of a fundamentalist Protestant church. They were apparently unaware that the storied Asoh—like the storied Jesus—was known for his commitments to forgiveness and, especially, to grace.

During the past few years, I have recounted the glorious story of Captain Asoh to managers from businesses, churches, academic institutions, and governmental organizations, and I have found that, apocryphal or not, the story has made Captain Asoh an instant folk hero of near-mythical stature. Although he is from another culture and was employed in a business with which most managers have little inside contact, his story has spoken to them.

Likewise, in my talks to managers, I have been impressed by the large number of people in my audiences who already know of Captain Asoh and also have heard the rumor that he committed suicide in the ultimate act of penance for his transgressions. Some have even reported reading newspaper articles describing his tragic act of despairing self-destruction. In fact, so many have reported his unseemly flight into that Ultimate Bay of Water—some with graphic descriptions of hara-kiri more reminiscent of *Shogun* than the front page of the *San Francisco Chronicle*—I felt compelled to check the validity of their reports with officials of the National Transportation Safety Board and Japan Air Lines. Some with whom I checked reported being aware of the rumor, but I was assured by all that Captain Asoh is alive and—contrary to our belief that organizational forgiveness is not possible—that he continued to fly for Japan Air Lines until his retirement a short time ago.

Regardless of his present employment status, Captain Asoh's spirit is still "flying the plane" for those who revere a symbol of reconciliation. In fact, given its durability and the character of the rumors and embellishments that surround it, the story of Captain Asoh runs the risk of falling into the same category of myth as the saga of Babe Ruth, who may or may not have "called his shot" prior to hitting his famous home run; the historical accounts of the Danish king who may or may not have offered to wear a yellow arm band as a means of defying the Nazis' attempts to deport Danish Jews; and the legend of Davy Crockett, who may or may not have died heroically in combat at the Alamo. Ultimately, I am saying that the story may not be factually true – but if it's not, why did we construct it, why do we want to believe it, why do we delight in it, and why do we say, "If it's not factual, it damn well ought to be"?

Whatever the facts of his statement in the hearing room, the truth is that the words attributed to Captain Asoh clearly touch, in a very powerful way, the nerve endings of a lot of people who live in a wide variety of organizations. Why is that so?

As I set about to answer my theoretical question, please keep in mind that I am discussing the Captain Asoh of the aforementioned story and not the Captain Asoh described in the *Aircraft Accident Report* (op cit.), although I suspect that the real Captain Asoh possesses many of the characteristics we attribute to him in our story.

Asoh Told the Truth, and We Are Starved for It

Captain Asoh expressed – in unequivocal, unambiguous terms – the truth as he knew it. Faced with circumstances in which many of us find that deception is the norm, he didn't lie. In accordance with Sissela Bok's definition of lying, he didn't make a statement with the express purpose of misleading another person or persons.[6] How refreshing!

For managers who report that deception is rewarded in their work;[7] for the 69 percent in a national poll who said that "over the last ten years, this country's leaders have consistently lied to the people";[8] for those who read and believe a newspaper column saying that "ninety percent of testimony by executive branch witnesses is removed from the precise truth in degrees varying from the most subtle unconscious nuance to the greatest and most deliberate distortion";[9] for those students in Harvard Business School who reported about a classroom exercise, "It seemed as if everyone was lying";[10] for those who have read and find plausible the work of Wilfred Bion, who contends that some forms of mental illness stem from the learned capacity to lie;[11] and for those who have digested the work of Chris Argyris, who asserts that valid data is a requirement for personal growth and organizational effectiveness[12] — Captain Asoh's comment must provide welcome, albeit vicarious, relief. In short, when one is starved for truth, the truth is especially friendly.

Truth is friendly because it provides the basis for human connection. It relieves our alienation from one another. It serves as an antidote to anaclitic depression, a form of melancholy caused by being psychologically separated from others upon whom we lean for basic emotional support.[13] And it reduces the probability that we will experience marasmus, the mental and physical "wasting away" that results when anaclitic depression is not relieved by attachment to others — an attachment that our relationship to truth facilitates.

Paradoxically, a small percentage of the population finds Asoh's truthful statement a source of threat, rather than a source of delight, reassurance, and security. For a long time, I have wondered why, and I think I now understand the reason. If Asoh had the courage to tell the truth and cope with whatever consequences resulted, the rest of us are confronted with a similar risky choice. We could be expected to tell the unadorned truth rather than lying when we are faced with answering important questions in our organizations. In the absence of the possibility of forgiveness, that is a risk many of us would prefer not to take.

Therefore, I suspect — although I have no scientific proof to verify my suspicions — that the persons made most uncomfortable by the mythic Asoh's assault on deception are the ones who also believe that Asoh committed suicide. In other words, if others will not destroy Asoh for us when he tells the truth, then we must believe that he destroyed himself. Believing that, we are released, at least in our minds, from the responsibility of speaking the truth when life offers us the same opportunity. Sadly, we also are released from sharing in the delight of interconnectedness.

He Had a Sense of Humor and a Capacity to Expose Obvious Absurdity

In what may appear to be another paradox, Asoh demonstrated a sense of humor and an appreciation of the absurd. These qualities not only were useful, but they also—unlike many other approaches to coping with life's problems—were healthy. George Vaillant, who did a long-term developmental study of the coping mechanisms of men, describes humor as "one of the truly elegant defenses in the human repertoire." Vaillant calls humor "one of mankind's most potent antidotes for the woes of Pandora's box." Although Vaillant conceded that humor was difficult to define, he described it as the "overt expression of ideas and feelings without individual discomfort or immobilization and without unpleasant effect on others," which, in turn, "lets you call a spade a spade. . . . [L]ike hope, humor permits one to bear and yet focus upon what is too terrible to be borne, . . . humor *never excludes* other people[14] [emphasis mine].

In a similar vein, Norman Cousins contends that humor has a healing quality to it. Cousins claims that he literally laughed his way out of a crippling disease his doctors believed to be irreversible and probably fatal.[15]

Whatever scientists or literati may tell us about a sense of humor, intuition tells me that it is important to individual and organizational effectiveness. I have never known a competent manager, leader, subordinate, colleague, teacher, preacher, parent, politician, or coach who didn't have a sense of humor or an appreciation of the absurd. Have you? Oddly, though, expression of humor is frequently discouraged in organizational settings. For instance, Michael Maccoby found that 53 percent of the managers he polled thought that a sense of humor was important for doing competent work, but only 14 percent of those managers felt that it was stimulated by work.[16]

Taking Maccoby's findings together with Vaillant's, you are left with the conclusion that in order to succeed, managers must give up one of the truly elegant means of coping. Or, as I said earlier, bullphrogs frequently die laughing, but steerphrogs seldom laugh. They just croak.[b] Captain Asoh was certainly no steerphrog; and we love him all the more for it.

Humor and absurdity also bind us together. If we can't express healing humor while at work, we can at least be grateful to Captain Asoh, who allows us to do it vicariously.

He Took Responsibility for His Own Actions but Not for the Actions of Others

A hoary homily of management is, "you can delegate authority, but you can't delegate responsibility." To the best of my understanding, that bureaucratic aphorism means that you are responsible for your own individual performance. In addition, though, you are responsible for causing your subordinates to perform. If they perform competently, you are the cause of their success. If they perform incompetently, you are the cause of their failure, too.

As evidence of that policy, I point to athletic coaches who routinely are fired if their teams don't win. Teachers, too, are held responsible for what their students learn; if they don't cause their students to learn enough to make certain scores on standardized tests, the teachers are fired. Regardless of their professions, leaders are held responsible for causing their subordinates' performances.

In very concrete terms, if subordinates perform well, the manager gets a bonus. If subordinates perform poorly, the manager gets fired, generally with the explanation, "You failed to motivate your people." The manager's job, then, seems to be to alter the subordinates in some way.[c] A disproportionate number of management education pro-

---

[b]For those who weren't reared in Texas, a steer is a castrated bull, and one way that managers are castrated (or involuntarily have their tubes tied) is to take away their sense of humor. Bullphrogs (managers with their sexual capacity intact) frequently die laughing, but steerphrogs seldom laugh. Steers don't have a lot to laugh about.

[c]I am always impressed by the word *alter* when used in the context of management and organization. I suppose one can make an argument for altering dogs and cats. One even might make a case for altering a rhinoceros if one has uncommon courage or limited mental acuity. If you alter people, though, you sterilize them—turning them into steerphrogs.

grams are designed to deal with leadership rather than followership. If organization members can be seduced into believing that leaders are more responsible than followers as causal factors in organizational success, then followers don't have to behave responsibly toward their leaders, toward one another, or toward their tasks as they go about their work. Subordinates are treated as nonentities. Given that, is it any wonder that followers become apathetic and nonproductive in any organization that denies their unique contribution?

For me, the subtly malignant consequence of accepting responsibility for others' actions is best demonstrated by the relationship between students and teachers, because it is a relationship most of us experience during our lifetime. Specifically, a common maxim implanted in the heads of many teachers is, "If the student hasn't learned, the teacher hasn't taught." Subjected to close scrutiny, that maxim involves a very perverse logic, because it implies that the basic responsibility for causing the student to learn belongs to the teacher. Like the management example, if the student does incompetent work, the teacher is assumed to be the cause and is held accountable for the student's incompetence. Following the same rationale rigorously, if the student does competent work, the teacher must get the credit for causing that, also. Thus, the student doesn't exist, except as a rather inanimate receptacle (some might say a chamber pot) for the teacher's competence or incompetence.

Is it any wonder that, relegated to being the effect of someone else's cause in the Great Classroom of Life, so many students become alienated and rebellious? Likewise, is it any wonder that, faced with such alienated rebelliousness, so many teachers burn out—also feeling alienated, rebellious, and guilt-ridden for failing to fulfill their responsibility to cause their students to perform at a level that either the teacher, the student, or someone else believes to be acceptable?

Likewise, politicians are held responsible for causing the behavior of their constituents. (The fact that we have destroyed, either metaphorically or actually, most of our presidents since Teddy Roosevelt, says much more about us than about the presidents we destroyed.) Thus, if the economy suffers from inflation, the president is held responsible for causing it, and we either oust him from office or take his life.

Parents—not God's providential will, the vagaries of the universe, genetic predispositions, or free choice—are considered responsible for causing their children's behavior. If their offspring behave badly, parents are made to feel guilty for their parental incompetence.[d] The list of supervisory responsibilities is apparently endless.

The relationships between managers and subordinates, teachers and students, elected officials and constituents, and parents and children have been called asymmetric relationships. These relationships are asymmetric because the distribution of powers and responsibilities is often lopsided in one direction or the other. (Remember, whining and passive aggression disproportionately confer power to subordinates, so power is not always lopsided in favor of the top dog.) When the participants in asymmetric relationships connive for the authority figure to assume all the responsibility, the leaders and followers are engaging in mutual destruction. To characterize such fruitless behavior, I have coined the term *parabiotic*. A combination of the words *parasitic* and *symbiotic*, the term describes a. comfortable, mutually destructive relationship—as when two leeches attach themselves to one another and proceed to suck one another dry.

Captain Asoh had the courage to pull the two leeches apart—by assuming responsibility for his own actions, nothing more and nothing less. In Argyris's terms, Captain Asoh "owned up."[17] He didn't blame the managers above him at Japan Air Lines; he didn't blame his flight crew; and he didn't blame the air traffic controllers. Nor did he absolve any of those parties of their particular responsibility when he said, "Asoh fuck up."

Accepting such a limited but realistic view of responsibility, Asoh again provided us with vicarious enjoyment. That enjoyment stems from seeing the possibility of being responsible for our own actions, whatever their quality might be, while at the same time being freed from the belief that we are responsible for causing the choices and

---

[d]I think it is very fortunate that parents are made to feel guilty or incompetent as the causes of their kids' problems. Otherwise, we psychologists and psychiatrists wouldn't have anyone to sit in our offices and purchase conversation for fifty-minute hours.

actions of others—a responsibility we know, deep down, that we can neither accept nor fulfill.

Captain Asoh Provided Us with the Opportunity to Meet Our Need to Express Altruism

Vaillant describes altruism as "getting pleasure from giving to others what you yourself would like to receive."[18] Through his implicit assumption that forgiveness and even grace were possible, Asoh provided us with the opportunity to meet our needs for altruism. Along with humor, altruism is one of the mature adaptations to life. As such, it provides a welcome alternative to its opposite—getting *pain* from taking from others what you yourself would rather not receive.

Whatever it is called, the expression of altruism is not only an experience that is existentially satisfying. It is also, as Edmund Wilson describes, a requirement for the survival of one's culture.[19] In fact, Wilson asserts that altruism is transferred genetically from generation to generation and that such transfer occurs because it has survival value. In more specific terms, cultures whose members express altruism in the form of forgiveness and grace survive. Cultures that lack the capacity for altruistic forgiveness and grace die.

Captain Asoh, in his statement of pithy reality, threw himself upon the mercy of the court and, by doing so, offered us the opportunity to express our innate altruism. Although we may not be aware of the reason for the pleasure we receive from his act, we are grateful to him for it.

Captain Asoh Opened the Opportunity for Organizational Grace

Finally, Captain Asoh offers those of us who live much of our lives in unforgiving, zero-defect organizations the hope that divine forgiveness, in the form of grace, will be woven into the everyday fabric of organizational life. Someday, for example, organizations will

1. Provide routine means to wipe the slate clean periodically, removing adverse personnel actions from employees' files[c]

2. Celebrate formal ceremonies of grace, designed to release members from the condition of eternal punishment so characteristic of contemporary organizations

3. Provide training programs that reacquaint and instruct us in the fine art of apology and in the more difficult art of learning to accept apologies—with grace

Then organizations will discover other ways to make forgiveness and grace—in both a secular and a spiritual sense—an integral part of our bureaucratic lives.

When that happens, the cloud of anaclitic depression and marasmus that hangs over our nonforgiving organizations will lift. Then we will emblazon in stone across the entrance portals of our places of work the good captain's immortal words, "Asoh fuck up"—not as an obscenity, but as a prayer that affirms both the best of our humanity and our potential for that which is truly divine.

---

[c]An example of such a routine process may be found in a recent contract negotiated between the Hotel Owners' Association and members of the Restaurant Employees' Union in Washington, D.C. According to the *Washington Post*:

> The contract change that brought the loudest response, besides the pay increase, was the Union's demand that disciplinary write-ups be destroyed after 18 months. No longer, Richardson explained to an excited crowd, could supervisors keep critical write-ups hanging over employees' heads forever. (P. Earley, "Hotel Employee Union Ratifies New Pact," *Washington Post*, 18 September 1981, B1)

6

Eichmann in the Organization

S OME time ago, in his role as a department head of a major mid-western university program, a colleague of mine—Ted—was approached by a member of the university's senate, who offered him the following proposition:

As you know, Ted, the university is in financial difficulty and is projecting an operating deficit for each of the following three years. In response to a request from the president, the Senate Committee on Finance and Administration has met and talked about a number of approaches for coping with the problem. After careful consideration of a variety of alternatives, we have decided that the quickest, most effective, and most realistic way to cope with the problem is to cut back on staff, since, as you know, the faculty code has a financial exigency clause which permits us to release even tenured faculty if we can prove their academic programs are not financially viable. And, as you also probably know, the College of Humanities is not pulling its weight. Consequently, here is what we want to do—and we will need your cooperation if the plan is to be carried out with minimum disruption to all involved. Given that any attempt to get rid of faculty, particularly those with tenure, will undoubtedly create an uproar, the president of the university, acting on the advice of our committee, is going to call for an across-the-board reduction in the faculty; and we want to support him with a vote of confidence in the Faculty Senate. That kind of consensual, democratic action should make everyone feel as if no one is being singled out or discriminated against. However, you people in the Business School, along with those in the School of Law, are the real money-makers in the university; so, if you go along with the vote, we will guarantee not to cut back on your faculty. In fact, we will work out a way, informally, of course, for you to add faculty. That should make everyone happy, except for the dead wood we get rid of. Naturally, they are going to complain. It's human nature, you know, to resist change. No matter how we do it, though, we intend to make their "outplacement" as painless as possible. We will give them at least a year's salary, as required by the school's governing code. We will also offer to help them get jobs somewhere else, although that probably isn't very realistic, since academic jobs are in short supply. We want them and everyone else to feel as if we are trying to help, though. Anyway, that is what we have in mind. Can we count on your cooperation?

As he listened to the proposition, Ted recalls that he suddenly thought of Hannah Arendt's classic book on organization and bureaucracy, *Eichmann in Jerusalem: A Report on the Banality of Evil.*[1] Ted thought of the collusive role played by the Jewish councils—the most powerful, respected, and trusted members of the Jewish community—in the liquidation of their own people, including, in the end, themselves.

According to Arendt, members of the councils closely cooperated in the destruction of their associates, colleagues, friends, and relatives through a variety of actions. For example, they compiled lists for the Nazis of persons to be deported. They secured money from deportees to pay the expenses related to their deportation and extermination. They distributed the yellow star badges and arm bands on behalf of the Nazis to potential deportees so that they could be identified easily when the "roundup" occurred. They collected the assets of those who were deported and turned those assets over to the Nazis. They served as police during the actual seizure of people and property. Finally, they made decisions about the minute minority who were to be saved—essentially, those who were the most community-oriented and the most prominent members of the faith.

As my friend looked into the face of the esteemed university senator who was presenting the proposition, he recounts, "I suddenly saw Adolph Eichmann, the banal bureaucrat, head of the Center for Emigration of Austrian Jews, standing before me. Although clothed in academic robes, the senatorial Eichmann was offering me an opportunity to join our own version of a Jewish council. In return, we would accrue the temporary rewards from the division of the assets of my deported colleagues in the College of Humanities."

The senator's request for cooperation and support further reminded Ted of Arendt's statement that the Nazis possessed neither the will power nor the manpower to remain "tough" when they met the determined opposition of the Danes to the Nazis' proposals relating to deporting the Jews from Denmark. When the Germans attempted to introduce the yellow badges to identify Danish Jews for deportation, they were told by the Danes that the king would be the first to wear one. In the same vein, influential officials of the Danish government, unlike the Norwegian Nazi collaborator Quisling, said that they would resign immediately if they observed any anti-Jewish acts by the Germans. Facing such unified opposition, the Germans failed, for all intents and purposes, in their attempt to export the Danish Jews. As Arendt so poetically put it: "They had met resistance based on 'principle,' and their 'toughness' had melted like butter in the sun."[2] In addition, as a result, a few of the Germans "had even been encouraged to express a few timid beginnings of genuine courage"[3] by communicating to their superiors their doubts and disagreements about the policy of deportation. In other words, the Danes' principled acts not only saved the majority of their Jewish citizenry but also freed some of the Germans to act with humane courage. Thus, the Danes' actions shifted—at least psychologically—from being solely acts of resistance to being acts that recognized and released their captors' nascent humanity.

Ted tells me that he suddenly realized that he was being propositioned—seduced, if you will—to join the university senators in a bureaucratic bed in which a kiss is not a preamble to producing a child of God but rather is the precursor to rape.

Reassured by that flash of insight, Ted replied: "No thanks. You cannot count on my cooperation. I don't send people to the gas chamber."

Not being illiterate, the senator knew immediately what Ted meant. His reply was one of instantaneous fury: "You surely don't really believe that there is any similarity between getting rid of a couple of dozen unproductive, dead-wood faculty members and shipping six million innocent people to their deaths in gas chambers, do you? What do you think I am? A murderer of some sort?"

At first Ted thought that the senator had a valid point. Perhaps Ted had been incorrect, unfair, unkind, and, ultimately, mean to his senatorial colleague. However, as he began to experience guilt at the thought of his unkind indiscretion, he also remembered the age-old parable of the man who was attempting to engage the services of a woman of the night. In the process of negotiating the fee, he offered her five dollars. In fury, she shouted, "Five dollars! What do you think I am? A common whore?" "That, Madam," he replied, "has already been established. All we are doing now is debating price."

Building upon the metaphor mixed in the blender of Ted's mind, he said, "That, Senator, has already been established, because if I go along with your proposal, all that will be left to debate is price. In fact, all I can think of to talk about now is how much of our colleagues' salaries will go to us, once we get them on the trains."

The senator again reacted with rage. Not only was he well-read, but he clearly also knew the parable of the woman of the night.

Then, in a reaction that Ted neither expected nor understood at the time, the senator's attitude quickly shifted from anger to poignant silence. After a moment, he said, "I'll be damned. You are right. We were about to 'sell them down the river.' I knew something was wrong with what we were doing. I just didn't know what. I'm going back to the committee and I'll tell them I think we are going about this the wrong way." Like the Nazis, his hard-nosed, intransigent managerial toughness melted like butter when confronted with opposition that was grounded in principle. As a consequence, he, too, was freed to behave morally. Much later, when Ted told me this story, he said, "I tell you, Jerry, the fact that he reversed himself shook me up. I have learned a lot from that—maybe more than I ever wanted to know."

The Story's Impact on Me

The full impact of my colleague's story did not hit me until I, too, read Arendt's work. The effect was particularly great when I came across Eichmann's bittersweet description of his birth: "I entered life on earth in the aspect of a human being."[4] Later, I learned that a half-dozen "unfriendly" psychiatrists who had interviewed him prior to his trial had described him as "normal." (One was reported to have said that he was "more normal, at any rate, than I am after having examined him.")[5] In addition, the psychiatrists concluded that he had a "desirable" attitude toward his family, his relatives, and his friends. In a similar manner, a minister who visited him regularly described him as "a man with positive ideas."[6] Faced with such information, I realized the clear possibility that—despite all his evil—Eichmann, like the university senator, had possessed a potential for moral, principled, compassionate behavior.

In fact, had he not possessed such a potential, no one could have accused him of being so immoral and evil, any more than one could accuse a water buffalo of immoral behavior for goring a child. It is only because Eichmann failed to exercise his human choice to behave morally that he is damnable.

Finally, as I read about Eichmann's life, I realized that I was unable to find a single recorded instance in his official SS career when a colleague, a subordinate, a friend, a family member, or an enemy confronted him directly with the immorality of his administrative actions. Likewise, no one reminded him of his potential choice to behave with rectitude. In fact, during his trial, Eichmann himself said that not a single person "came to me and reproached me for anything in the performance of my duties."[7] According to Arendt's account, neither friend nor foe contradicted him on that point.

I wonder why so many people lacked the sense of principle or moral courage to confront him in that way. I also wonder why my colleague Ted, faced with similar generic circumstances, chose the alternative of expressing his respectful humanity and love, both to the members of the senate and to his colleagues in the School of Humanities, most of whom he did not know personally.

The answers to those questions as well as the conclusion to the story are very important. I have checked with my colleague, and I announce with relief and pride that the senator's reevaluation of his position, my friend's principled opposition, the principled opposition of others, or all of those events in combination saved the sacrificial humanities professors from professional extermination. In fact, despite the dire prophecies of financial collapse, the university has survived. It has survived even though each of those in its employ probably is making a little less money than he or she would be making had the spoils of a mass deportation been divided among the survivors. In addition, many members of the university community seem to share a sense of growing pride in and commitment to the institution because, like the Danes, they stuck together during a time of organizational crisis.

Since my friend recited the parable of the faculty senator, I have realized that by participating in an organization's disloyalty to peers and selfish collusion, we prostitute our souls. By doing so, we destroy the delicate threads of human fabric that are required not only to make those organizations function effectively but also to allow them to survive. Furthermore, it is my belief that such moral auctions did not begin or end with Adolph Eichmann, his colleagues, the Jewish councils, or those who died at Auschwitz and other Nazi death camps.

In fact, although the evil enormity of the Holocaust can never be overlooked, that generic pattern of villainy is not unique to Eichmann or to those who colluded with him. It is practiced daily in formal organizations of all kinds. Adolph Eichmann, the Jewish councils, and those we designate as their victims did not have aberrant values and thought patterns. If you don't believe that, ask the despairing, dispirited men and women who have been laid off, terminated, fired, or RIFed from General Motors, the U.S. Government, a university, or Maudine's Grocery Store and Skating Palace what the experience was like for them. Listen to their anger, their frustration, their depression, and their bitterness. Likewise, listen to those from the same organizations, who, frequently against their better judgment and will, have managed the terminations and RIFs. In general, few are overwhelmed with gratitude for the experience. Participating in evil deeds doesn't seem to be much fun for anyone.

A Jewish colleague who read a draft of this chapter initially viewed the analogy between facilitating an RIF and colluding with Eichmann as a trivialization of the Holocaust. At first I considered scrapping this chapter, because there is no comparison between being burned in

Nazi crematoria and being unjustly fired by a corporation. But my Jewish colleague and I both recalled that the Holocaust began with seemingly minor acts of unjust discrimination—such as the issuance of Jewish ID cards. When the Jewish councils acquiesced to—even assisted the implementation of—that sort of relatively minor outrage, the population of Germany and the officials of the Reich began the relentless climb up the ladder toward psychological readiness to commit genocide. The incremental escalation of human rights violations also prepared the victims to accept their victimization, in a process that Bruno Bettelheim termed "identification with the aggressor."[8]

Perhaps the error resides in trivializing emotionally disruptive calamities, such as an unjust RIF. For that reason, it is a heroic act to make a mountain out of a molehill and—like Ted—to refuse to join your organization's equivalent of a Jewish council. It is easy to see a partisan who blows up a Nazi munitions train as a hero; it is more difficult to see the Jewish community leader who refused to facilitate the assignment of ID numbers as a hero. And it is still more difficult to see a recalcitrant faculty senator as a hero. It requires true moral resolve and clear thinking to recognize a tiny atrocity and nip it in the bud. The more we discussed the issues raised by Ted's story, the more my Jewish colleague and I agreed that it is important to publish that message.

Given the pervasiveness of thought that leads to seduced collusion, to assert that the actions taken by the Jewish councils were unique to the Jews is a subtle act of anti-Semitism. Likewise, to assume that the value system and thought pattern underlying the callous inhumanity of Adolph Eichmann and his associates is unique to the Germans is an equally subtle act of anti-Teutonism. Ask Pol Pot's victims in the "killing fields" of Cambodia if the qualities required for holocausts are unique to Germany. Both the Jewish councils and the Eichmanns who made up the Center for Emigration of the Austrian Jews are common bureaucratic artifacts. They are created and perpetuated by those of us who play a set of roles and apply a pattern of thought in order to build and maintain organizations of all kinds. Those roles and thought patterns, in turn, occur in profit-making companies, Christian churches, government agencies, universities, and voluntary associations. They are the basis of collusion with institutional evil. And none of us – myself included – can deny that he or she might participate as the victimizer or as the traitor who facilitates the victimization of others.

Organizational Murder

An RIF, then, is a step in the direction of a holocaust. In the words of Jules Feiffer, an RIF is a "little murder."[9] What are the dynamics of the collusion that leads organization members to murder each other?

The practice of collusion seems to require several structural elements: consenting parties who play predetermined roles, a justifying theory, and a variety of shared mental tricks to maintain that theory when faced with the tremendous internal pressure to surrender it. Such internal pressure is frequently called the impact of conscience.

I should add that the presence of formal organization does not imply that collusion in atrocities is inevitable. Bureaucracy, according to Jaques,[10] sometimes produces trust, confidence, and love. At other times it produces distrust, alienation, and paranoia. Which it produces depends on how we construct it and the consequent actions we take, day by day, as we work within it.

Consenting Parties Who Play Predetermined Roles

Consenting parties are a requirement for collusion to occur. These consenting parties collude in playing predetermined roles. As Arendt suggests, the roles, with one major exception, are not unlike the roles in a traditional play. The exception stems from the fact that in Eichmann-style organizational collusion, there are no heroes or protagonists in the usual sense of the word. There are only victims, who suffer like the leeches that suck each other dry in a "parabiotic" relationship. (I defined my term *parabiotic* in the preceding chapter.)

Basically, though, several roles (or jobs) must be carried out if all members are to suffer appropriately and, by doing so, are to perform the service of directing the play of organizational passions to its tragic conclusion.

The Top Management Villain. The top management villain is played by the person who, in the traditional view of leadership, is generally believed to be responsible for causing the violence, whatever form it may take. (As many of us know, a leader can delegate authority but cannot delegate responsibility.) As described by Arendt, that role was played by Hitler, Himmler, and a few other prominent Nazis.

In other formal organizations, that role in firing (or terminating or RIFing) people is generally performed by individuals with such titles as CEO, president, dean, bishop, or general. Sometimes, top management villains post the slogan of their role on their desks: "The buck stops here."

Regardless of their disparate job titles, the villains are united by the fact that the order to fire people is issued in their names. Furthermore, they order that others be fired for the purpose of suiting the selfish interests of those who remain, not because the "firees" have performed incompetently or immorally.

To fully understand the role, one must realize that top management villains act out their roles in unconscious obedience to the wishes of the majority of the other members of the organizations that they ostensibly are leading. By doing so, they serve as convenient scapegoats, whose callousness protects their constituents from the fury of those who play the roles of victims. More important, having a villain to blame makes it easier for the rest of us to escape the reality of our complicity in sanctioning the murder.

Few top management villains enjoy the role. Those who do enjoy it are truly evil. Most perform the role in the mistaken notion that they have no alternatives. Perhaps, someday, they will recognize that, like the Danes, they have the alternative of acting with humane consideration; when they do, they will become top management heroes.

The Middle Management Executioners. The middle management executioners are assigned the role of middlemen (or "middlepeople") in executing policy that they did not mandate. Played by Eichmann in Arendt's description, the role requires slavish obedience to a "godfather-like" figure. That role is somewhat akin to the one played by participants in Milgram's famous experiment in which individuals were instructed to deliver what they believed to be painful electrical shocks to unwilling victims.[11] Milgram reported that up to 65 percent of the participants delivered such shocks simply because a person in a position of authority commanded them to do so. He also reported that many did it despite strong personal reservations about their actions. Some even administered the shocks believing the victim to be in extreme danger.

Because of the executioners' intermediate role, it is difficult for the victims to attribute their destruction to them unequivocally. For instance, during his trial, Eichmann contended, with exasperating justification, that he did not commit murder alone but was an accessory to the murders that were committed, in which many others, especially his superiors and the Jewish councils, played important contributory roles. Because of the glimmers of truth it contained, this argument was not an easy one with which to cope, even for those who played the role of victim.

Thus was the Eichmann defense born. And thus does it live today in the actions of people such as Ted's senator.

The Policy Implementors. Policy implementors are those who actually carry out (as opposed to manage) the atrocity. In what might appear to be an anomaly, those who actually implement the policy are generally chosen because they have no genuine commitment to the task and gain no enjoyment from it. For example, when selecting SS personnel to carry out the task of extermination, "systematic effort was made to weed out all those who derived physical pleasure from what they did."[12]

The SS personnel are not alone in the distaste they have for their job. In a variety of formal organizations, one hears, again and again, "The hardest thing I have ever had to do was to hand out RIF notices" or "You don't know what misery is until you have to let some of your people go" or "The toughest part of being a supervisor is handling terminations." Occasionally, one even overhears a face-to-face conversation: "Sorry, John, old friend. I really don't want to let you go, but I have no choice. I just got a direct order from Headquarters to cut back 10 percent on personnel; so despite your excellent work, your loyal service, our long friendship and the many good times we have had together, I have to give you a pink slip." (In one organization, it was a yellow arm band. Whatever the color or shape, the symbolic meaning is the same.)

Because of their obvious distaste for the job, even the victims fail to blame those who actually carry out the atrocity. The guilty party is always difficult to identify when viewed in the poor light of an organization in which moral darkness prevails. Since nobody and everybody is responsible for the crimes of bureaucracies, Arendt characterizes bureaucratic activities as "rule by nobody."

Implementor's Assistants. For an organization to engage in systematic villainy, perpetrators and victims alike need the assistance of professionally trained experts if they are to function in a manner they mistakenly believe to be both efficient and humane.

Medical doctors provided that professional expertise in Eichmann's world. Using their professional skills, these physicians developed what they contended was a humane way of killing, one that granted deportees what they termed a "mercy death." They not only devised it, they also supervised it, and they were governed by the belief that the "unforgivable sin was not to kill people, but to cause unnecessary pain."[13]

Members of the personnel department usually perform this assistant's role in organizations involved in less malignant forms of termination. Sometimes the role is performed by professional consultants with a variety of euphemistic job titles, such as "outplacement specialist," "separation counselor," or "downsizing facilitator." Like the physicians, their job is not to question the efficacy or morality of the RIF; their job is to facilitate it in a way that causes the least possible amount of pain to those who are terminated.

Early Victims. Early victims are those who are the first to go. They were the mentally ill and physically infirm in Germany. They were the Jews who were deported first from Poland, France, and Belgium. They were the first hourly workers laid off by Chrysler. They were the employees of the U.S. Government who received the first RIF notices in the interoffice mail. They were the janitorial workers at American University, Washington, D.C., who were the first victims of the moves announced by its president. Early victims tend to be the weakest in terms of formal power.

The complicity of early victims in their own demise is quite subtle. About all one usually can do is ask sympathetically, as Jews have asked their surviving relatives, "Why didn't you revolt and charge and attack?"[14] or, as children of deposed employees of contemporary organizations will probably ask their parents, "Why didn't you sue or strike or tear the place apart?" Then, whoever asks the question generally feels sorry that such victims were so impotent in their plight. Although historians tend to accord early victims more sympathy and pity, such victims, in the final analysis, are neither metaphorically nor actually less dead.

Later Victims. Playing a key role, later victims are those who collude most directly with their victimizers. In their complicity, they play a role similar to that described by Winston Churchill in the early stages of World War II when he warned of the dire fate that awaited those who sought to appease Hitler. Said he, "Each one hopes that if he feeds the crocodile enough, the crocodile will eat him last. All hope the storm will pass before their turn comes to be devoured."[15]

This role—perhaps the most disturbing one identified during Eichmann's trial—was played by members of the Jewish councils. The councils were composed of the most prominent and powerful members of the Jewish community. According to Arendt:

> Without Jewish help in administrative and police work . . . there would have been either complete chaos or an impossibly severe drain on German manpower. There can be no doubt that without the cooperation of the [later] victims, it would hardly have been possible for a few thousand people [the Germans], most of whom, moreover, worked in offices, to liquidate many hundreds of thousands of other people.[16]

Members of the Jewish councils who provided such administrative and police assistance were given tremendous powers by the Nazis, but only on a short-term basis. Ultimately, they were also deported and killed. In Arendt's words:

Even the members of the Jewish councils were invariably exterminated. . . . There were no exceptions, for the fate accorded the slave laborers was only a different, slower kind of death.[17]

During RIFs, the role of later victims, ostensibly the most powerful members of the victim class, is frequently played by union officers, faculty senators, or management representatives with the well-known title "hatchet men." Whatever their titles, they actively assist the more powerful villains, executioners, implementors, and assistants in the process of locating and terminating "early victims." In the course of their complicity, they frequently negotiate—even demand—that the order of deportation be expressed in the form of seniority rules. Thus, union leaders, usually those with the greatest amount of seniority, actually dictate the order of the march, with themselves, the most powerful and respected members of the union, going last.

Final Victims. Final victims have two distinguishing characteristics. First, they suffer as victims, but their victim status is not always recognized by historians. Second, they suffer as double victims. Not only are they victims of an injustice, but they also are victims of our need to imprison them in a role that diverts us from the difficult task of exploring our complicity in the particular crime from which they suffered. Thus, we, also, are deterred from examining our own potential complicity in future crimes.

The final victim classification includes one group that is generally cursed as persecutors—individuals such as Eichmann. For participating in atrocities, his neck was stretched on the gallows no less than his soul was shrunk at his desk. He, too, paid a high price for his participation in his organization's misdeeds. But who weeps for him? Indeed, who can make the *superhuman* effort to weep for Eichmann? But do we also fail to extend *human* compassion to perpetrators of lesser crimes? By comparison with the felonies of an Eichmann or a Pol Pot, the managers who mandate, manage, and implement corporate RIFs are commiting mere misdemeanors. Yet they also suffer from the damage they do both to others and to themselves. Although we love to hate them, I have met few persons who play that role and enjoy it. Most detest it. For that reason, they indeed need the anesthesia of "bullets to bite." Even though the pain they suffer is self-inflicted and much less obvious than that of their victims, it is no less real. Perhaps *some* victimizers could be forgiven if we had the ability to extend that level of grace.

Frequently acclaimed for their heroic survival, the second group of final victims includes those who spend the remainder of their lives consumed by hatred and frequently focused on achieving revenge for the wrongs they and other victims have suffered. To me, such victims are the most poignant. Sometimes members of the Jewish community, sometimes members of the management team, sometimes members of the labor council, sometimes members of the faculty union, they are united by the following statements:

> We suffered as victims at the hands of the victimizers. Since you did not suffer, you cannot understand. Furthermore, the fact that you did not suffer and cannot understand means that you cannot legitimately explore the nature of *our* complicity in the particular crime we suffered. Unfortunately, if you cannot discuss *our* collusion, you cannot understand *your* potential for future complicity; but we are willing to sacrifice your understanding to minimize our "survivor's guilt." Our relationship as unforgiving adversaries of the victimizers must continue, and you must not interfere with it.

In one sense, the final victims have taken the well-known epigram, "Those who are ignorant of history are doomed to repeat it," and have changed it to read, "Those who study history must interpret it in a particular way. Otherwise, they might understand their potential to repeat it."

Evidently we need to have final victims. So long as they continue in their role as unforgiving, vigilant victims, we do not have to explore the nature of *our* complicity. As prisoners of the cosmology of roles and thought patterns that led to their victimization, and as prisoners of our implicit encouragement for them to occupy those roles, they allow us to avoid the awesome truth stated by Shakespeare: "The fault, dear Brutus, lies not in our stars, but in ourselves." More tragically, by perpetuating the roles in the evil drama, we never get the opportunity to express and experience our extraordinary ability for love.

Assuming that we seek such an opportunity and frequently don't achieve it, the question then becomes, "Why?" What is the pattern of thought, carried by those final victims, that not only leads us to collude with evil but also prevents us from experiencing the ecstasy of love?

Thought Patterns That Facilitate Complicity

Once we opt to participate in a little murder, such as an RIF, we must learn and adopt a thought pattern, which we share with others, with which we can justify to ourselves and others our respective roles in the process.[a] That shared thought pattern includes an encompassing theory, euphemisms, slogans and clichés, negative fantasies, inner emigration, protective rules and regulations, selective memory, and lying. All elements of the pattern have the same function: to make life tolerable for those bound together by a common bond of loneliness and depression, generated by self-destructive, parabiotic collusion.

An Encompassing Theory. The theory's purpose is to justify collusion in the murderous process. That theory, in turn, must be broad enough to include both victims and victimizers in its Judas's kiss.

In Eichmann's Jerusalem (used in the metaphorical sense), the comprehensive theory revolved around an abiding belief in the state, its laws, and the consequent duties of a law-abiding citizen. Thus, Adolph Eichmann could do his duty to the state, obey the law, plead what came to be known as the Eichmann defense, and yet be destroyed by his slavish devotion to that theory. Likewise, at the same time—and also slavishly believing in the primacy of the state—Jews

---

[a]It is important to emphasize that the pattern is shared. Thus, the pattern differs from what psychoanalytic theorists refer to as defenses, which are individual, not collective, in nature.

volunteered for deportation and execution. Those who tried to warn them about the terrors that awaited them if they cooperated with both Jewish and Nazi agents of the state were denounced as insane.[18]

The overriding theory used by many U.S. organizations to justify the inhumanity of firing, axing, cutting, reducing, sacking, and terminating *others* is provided by economists who advise us "about the inevitability of the Phillips Curve—that is, that we have to accept high levels of unemployment in order to lower the rate of inflation."[19] Once we accept that theory, we can cut others from the work force without considering either the ethical or the moral implications. We can do so despite the fact that the economists, who play the role of implementor's assistants, "seldom make the point that each country has a different Phillips curve, with ours being one of the worst. No one seems to ask, 'Why?' "[20] Specifically, no one seems to ask why both the Japanese and the West Germans provide far more job security than we and have consistently outperformed us in both productivity and the control of inflation.

Few of us care to look at a Phillips curve for what it is: an expression of the amount of greed and inhumanity a culture can tolerate before it disintegrates. Thus, by providing a theoretical justification for RIFs, economists have joined sociologists, psychologists, and management theorists as apologists for the little murders that prepare us to commit the big ones.

Euphemisms. The purpose of euphemisms is to hide from oneself and others the unpleasant reality of what one is experiencing or doing. In Eichmann's world, the essence of euphemistic thinking was embodied in the "Language Rule," which referred to "what in ordinary language would be called a lie."[21] Under the Language Rule, words such as *killing*, *murder*, and *liquidation* were replaced in the Nazi vocabulary with words such as *final solution*, *evacuation*, and *special treatment*.

Profit-making organizations, such as the Equitable Life Assurance Company, fire long-term, faithful employees and euphemistically call the process "outplacement."[22] Among employees of the federal government, the firing of others is referred to in polite company as "reductions in force" (RIFs). Academic institutions employ a more complex euphemism; when we fire a colleague, we call it "giving him or her a terminal contract." Not only do we euphemistically describe the act as a gift, but we frequently attempt to plug the leaks in our moral dikes by "honoring" the soon-to-be-departed with a cynical ceremony euphemistically called a "going-away party." In an attempt to fully divert ourselves from the reality that the ceremony attempts to hide, we generally read a resolution praising him or her for "meritorious service to the faculty and students."

Although we may laugh at our use of euphemistic "bureau-babble," most of us are painfully aware of its malignant, deceptive purpose — to protect members of the bureaucracy from the reality of the tragedy in which they are participating. Paraphrasing a *Time* magazine article on "bureaucrateze," engaging in compensated genital pleasuring with a strolling free-lance orgasmetrician requires no exploration of the depths of our respective souls.[23]

Slogans and Clichés. Slogans and clichés are in the same genre of deception as euphemisms. *Webster's Seventh New Collegiate Dictionary* defines slogans as "brief striking phrases used in advertising or promotion" and clichés as "trite expressions" of the "ideas expressed by them."

Slogans and clichés can either express reality or disguise it. Within organizations, slogans and clichés lead us away from essence and reality. They deflect us from expressions of altruism, which Vaillant believes individuals and all human organizations require if they are to survive.[24]

If we are morally upright, we might ask our organizational bedfellows, "Why are you asking me to do something dishonorable, immoral or illegal?" They might reply with a slogan/cliché such as "My honor is my loyalty" — the slogan of the SS, coined by Hitler and used by Himmler in an apparent attempt to gloss over the enormity of the crimes they asked their people to commit. Others might shout, "Wear It with Pride, the Yellow Star!" a slogan created in 1933 by Robert Welthch, a Jewish journalist, in an effort to squelch thoughtful dissent by members of the Jewish community who questioned the efficacy of their leaders' commitment to the Zionist movement.[25] Some might mumble, "When the going gets tough, the tough get going" — John

Mitchell's stock reply to subordinates who questioned the morality of some of the actions taken in conjunction with the Watergate break-in. Occasionally, a manager might refer to the need to "come right with people"—a slogan/cliché used by President Coy Eklund in an apparent effort to justify to himself and others the "outplacement" of several hundred long-term employees of the Equitable Life Assurance Company.[26] Now and then, you might even hear a guilt-ridden administrator say, "Occasionally in this job I just have to 'bite the bullet,'"—a university dean's response to a question about why a faculty member was fired from a job in which he or she was doing well.

Such slogans and clichés frequently inhibit organization members from pursuing the essence of important ideas, questions, or moral issues. In addition, the slogans and clichés sometimes are used in a manner that distorts their original meanings. "To bite the bullet" is a good example. Originally, that phrase was meant to describe a realistic way to make pain bearable for someone who was to undergo surgery without the aid of anesthesia. Now it is used to connote a way to reduce the "heroic" suffering of the person who inflicts the pain. Thus, when a university dean says, "I must bite the bullet" (that is, fire an innocent person), it is similar to a surgeon saying, "I'm going to cut this man's leg off without using an anesthetic. God! The pain will be excruciating. You'd better give me a bullet to bite while I saw."

Whenever the language of slogans and clichés is employed and *we reply in kind*, we know that we have signed a contract with the devil.

Negative Fantasies. As I mentioned in the chapter about the Abilene Paradox, another justification we use to numb the pain of participating in villainy is the fantasy of disastrous consequences if we behave morally and sensibly.

Armed with negative fantasies, Eichmann could plead that he had no choice but to obey orders. Had he not done so, he believed and/or claimed that he would have been forced to commit suicide or, by implication, would have been executed for insubordination.[27] Neither fantasy was grounded in reality. Rather, as Arendt recounts, it was surprisingly easy "for members of extermination squads to quit without serious consequence for themselves"[28] In fact, "not a single case could be traced in which an SS member suffered the death penalty because of a refusal to take part in an execution."[29]

The use of negative fantasies is not limited to victimizers. For instance, Jewish collaborators frequently contended that they had cooperated with the Nazis in deporting fellow Jews so that they could avert more serious consequences—presumably, their own deaths. Thus, Dr. Rudolph Kastner, a Jewish collaborator, contended that he withheld information from doomed Jews scheduled for "deportation" because of "'humane' considerations, such as that 'living in the expectation of death by gassing would only be harder.'"[30]

Paradoxically, both Eichmann and Kastner—one an implementor and the other a victim—employed the same thought pattern and thus became the strangest of bedfellows.

Like Eichmann, most people engaged in villainy can produce convincing negative fantasies on demand. Thus, CEOs can argue, "The company will go bankrupt and everyone will lose his job if we don't get rid of the dead wood." Labor leaders can portend, "We will all lose our jobs if we don't toss those with low seniority overboard." Union members who are allowed to stay temporarily in the lifeboat can say, "Sorry. It is necessary to throw you over the side. That is the only way to save the majority of the crew."

Whether they are produced by CEOs, university presidents, union officials, faculty members, Jewish officials, or members of the SS, it is important that the purpose of negative fantasies be understood. If I, who have them, can convince you to believe they are true, then I am released in both our minds from any personal responsibility for solving the problems in an alternative realistic manner. Furthermore, once you believe them, you, too, have been seduced into collusion.

Inner Emigration. Some active participants in the Holocaust contended later that they had inwardly opposed it. This rationale for complicity has been termed *inner emigration,* and such inner emigrants frequently appeared more Nazi than the "real ones."[31] Like Poor Judd in the musical comedy *Oklahoma,* inner emigrants "loved everybody and everything. They just never let on." That which Shames has called "a crime of silence"[32] is one manifestation of such emigration.

Arendt—incorrectly, I believe—reserves the term to describe only members of the Third Reich who inwardly believed that certain behaviors were wrong, immoral, and evil but outwardly acted another way. Unlike Arendt, I contend that inner emigration occurs among all who participate in immoral activity. For example, the Jewish officials who were, in effect, extensions of the Jewish councils, became inner emigrants when they participated in the roundup of their fellow Jews. Arendt described one such emigrant who attempted to justify his cooperation with the Nazis in rounding up Jews for deportation by asserting "that Jewish policemen would be 'more gentle and helpful' and would 'make the ordeal easier' (whereas, in fact, they were, of course, more brutal and less corruptible, since so much was at stake for them)."[33]

Inner emigration also occurs in traditional organizations. It occurs when we are joined by an emigrant colleague as we leave a staff meeting, and he or she puts an arm around our shoulder and says: "I loved the way you argued with the boss in there. You said just what I wanted to say. I was tempted to help you out, but you said it so well I didn't think there was any need for me to comment. I want you to know, though, that I was with you all the way despite my silence. Incidentally, I'm sorry about your being fired for raising hell. I hope you find another job soon, and do let me know if you need to talk with someone. I'm an excellent listener."

Inner emigration is also the process by which individuals frequently justify succumbing to conformity pressures from superiors or colleagues. For instance, managers use inner emigration to justify giving pink slips to employees who they do not believe deserve them. Teenagers use the process to justify "ripping off" stores in response to peer pressures. It is the process by which lonely, insecure cowboys attempt to explain their participation in hangings they oppose, such as the one described in poignant detail in *The Ox-Bow Incident*.[34] It is also a way in which reluctant virgins of both genders lose their innocence in organizations, contending all along that they did it against their wills.

Rules and Regulations. Rigid adherence to rules and regulations—of which laws are a special category—is also used to justify our complicity in evil. Slavish obedience to rules and regulations is one way to avoid discomforting thoughts about our actions.

Espousing his faith in the sanctity of rules and regulations, Eichmann contended that he simply followed orders and did his duty as a law-abiding citizen of the state. As an adherent to the same faith, the personnel director of Ajax Corporation can contend that he simply followed the orders of the CEO when he distributed the pink slips. Likewise, the faculty senator can reply to the complaints of deposed faculty members that he was simply following the dictates of the faculty governing body.

Ultimately, though, a temporary escape into the fantasized protective custody of pseudocivilized rules and regulations only delays the moment at which the ultimate payment occurs. That defense didn't wash for Eichmann, and it didn't exonerate Lieutenant Calley and Captain Medina of their personal responsibility for the My Lai massacre in Vietnam.

Selective Memory. Selective memory—or, more accurately, selective forgetfulness—is another mental trick used to evade culpability. Eichmann was known for his inability to recall the essence of events in which he played a role that by any reasonable criterion would be called evil. However, he could remember the most mundane details of situations that enhanced his sense of status or his perverted sense of self-esteem. Thus, he could remember his visit with the minister of the interior of the Slovakian puppet government because he considered it a great honor to receive social invitations from high officials. He could even remember the way they bowled, the manner in which drinks were served, and other inconsequential details of the visit. He could not remember, however, that the purpose of the visit was to discuss the deportation of the Jews from Slovakia.[35]

Similarly, Jewish council members testifying at Eichmann's trial had great difficulty remembering the details of their own and others' collusion with the Nazis. However, they could remember, in excruciatingly painful detail, how Eichmann and his associates participated in the same events.

Once again, though, key figures in the Holocaust are not the only ones who suffer from selective memory. During the Watergate hearings and trials, the "I don't recall" replies of H.R. Haldeman and John Ehrlichman achieved the status of a national joke.

At first, I doubted that Eichmann, the Jewish council members, and Haldeman and Ehrlichman were telling the truth. Like many others, I was convinced that they could recall the details of events they professed to have forgotten. However, now I have had the opportunity to interview my colleague's co-worker—the university senator who wanted to fire the "dead wood." I trust the senator's veracity about the incident, and I am now convinced that he and the witnesses to other greater crimes truly have forgotten their own guilty deeds. I discovered that the senator, like Eichmann, could remember many inconsequential details about his conversation with my colleague; he could remember where they stood, the content of a meeting he had attended immediately prior to the conversation, and the weather conditions. Yet he could not remember many of the details of the conversation regarding the proposal to terminate his colleagues in the School of Humanities. In his words: "That was a painful time for me. One I would rather forget."

Psychiatrists frequently call such selective forgetfulness "repression." I call it a way to avoid the reality of the parabiotic relationship in which one has participated.

Lying. To avoid ultimately confronting culpability, many of us resort to lying. Sissela Bok defines a lie as "any intentionally deceptive message which is stated."[36] Arendt, however, expands the meaning of lying to include self-deception, which includes efforts to deceive oneself in the apparent service of survival. From Arendt's description, it is clear that lying was endemic to *all* parties involved in Eichmann's metaphorical Jerusalem. The Jews no less than the Nazis practiced both forms of lying. Of the two, I suspect (and Arendt implies) that self-deception plays a more destructive part in collusion with evil.

In Arendt's words, the "German society of eighty million people had been shielded against reality and factuality by . . . the same self-deception, lies and stupidity that had now become ingrained in Eichmann's mentality."[37] Simultaneously, self-deception was practiced by Jews who "volunteered for deportation from Theresienstadt to Auschwitz and denounced those who tried to tell the truth as being 'not sane.' "[38]

Such lying—to oneself and to others—is endemic among members of different kinds of organizations involved in parabiotic evil. For example, Mr. Coy Eklund, president of the Equitable Life Assurance Society, apparently employed both forms of deception when he pronounced his commitment to the policy of "coming right with people" and then proceeded to fire a number of loyal, long-term employees.[39] Or, describing our need to deceive ourselves, Zandy Leibowitz, a psychologist involved in RIF counseling says, "Crazy or not, people become frozen . . . Until you have a specific RIF notice in your hand, the way you get up and go to work every morning is to pretend it isn't happening."[40]

The ability to lie to ourselves and others can be learned so well that we may lose our awareness that we are doing it. Wilfred Bion, for one, contends that certain forms of mental illness may stem from learning to lie.[41] More directly, he contends that we sometimes learn to lie so skillfully that we can no longer differentiate a lie from the truth.

Whatever roles or mental patterns we may employ under the banal but evil covers of the bureaucratic bed, the implications are profound. They are profound because they comprise an approach to living that, over time, dulls one's moral sensibilities and decreases the probability of our individual and collective survival. As the Nazis knew so well, the roles and mental patterns generate a "system which succeeds in destroying its victim before he mounts the scaffold," a system which "is incomparably the best for keeping a whole people in slavery. In submission."[42]

Getting Eichmann out of the Organization

Is there any alternative? Inevitably, are all formal organizations versions of the hell that Eichmann symbolizes? Particularly during times of economic crisis, must organizations engage in the form of collusive murder that we euphemistically call RIFs?

As far as I am concerned, the answer to those rhetorical questions is no. That unequivocal response stems from my emerging understanding of the heroic role played by the Danes when they resisted the Nazis' attempts to seduce them into colluding in the deportation of Jews. When the Nazis were confronted with such resistance, "the result seems to have been that those exposed to it *changed their minds*. They had met resistance based on *principle* . . . and had been able to show a few timid beginnings of genuine courage"[43] (emphasis mine).

Danish resistance virtually defeated the Nazis' effort to deport Jews from Denmark. The Danes' resistance also was, paradoxically, an expression of affirming love toward the Nazis as well as toward one another. It was an expression of love because it increased the probability that *all* potential victims—including Jews, gentile Danes, Nazis, and others—would survive. By refusing to collude in the RIF of their Jewish citizenry, the Danes engaged in lovemaking in its most comprehensive sense.

Encouraged by the Danes' capacity for expressing love under such trying circumstances, I am convinced that all organizations have potential "Danish lovemakers." Those 'lovemakers" have both the capacity and the desire to express affectionate concern toward one another, despite pressure caused by the reality of limited material resources. Not only can they express such concern, but they can do it in a way that increases the probability that the organization will survive and flourish.

The question then becomes, "How do they do it?" In particular, "How do they do it during hard times, when the temptation to terminate others' employment is great?" Well, as I think about that question, I am not sure *how* they do it, but I do have some thoughts about *what* they have to do if their relationship to one another is going to be one of love, rather than villainy. In short, I have some thoughts about how to get Adolph Eichmann out of the organization and to replace him with some "Danes."

The Dynamics That Lead to Collusion with Evil

Carl Jung contended that any dimension of human behavior can also be expressed in its opposite form. If we follow Jung's contention, then the same fuel that fired the ovens of Auschwitz must have provided the fiery energy of love that allowed the Danes to say no to the Nazis. Likewise, the fuel that stokes the layoffs at "Universal Industries" must also stoke the fate-sharing behavior of Japanese workers who take proportional pay cuts rather than permitting their associates to join the march to the metaphorical ovens of unemployment.[44]

Arendt asserts that the dynamics of the Holocaust stemmed from a universal instinct. She describes that instinct as "the animal pity by which all normal men are affected in the presence of physical suffering." Building upon that possibility, Arendt continues:

> The *trick* [emphasis mine] used by Himmler . . . was very simple . . . and effective; it consisted in turning these instincts around, as it were, in directing them toward the self. So that instead of saying: What horrible things I did to people!, the murderers would be able to say: What horrible things I had to watch in the pursuance of my duties, how heavily the task weighed upon my shoulders!"[45]

I think Arendt is correct when she contends that a universal instinct was involved. I do not believe it was animal pity, however. Rather, I think that the dynamics of villainy are associated with our instinctive need for attachment and support from others whom we trust and the reciprocal fear that our need for attachment will be violated by separation.

Each of us, as a condition of existence, fears separation from and seeks attachment to others. Coping successfully with these reciprocal desires leads to love. Failing to cope with them successfully leads to hate and chicanery. That generalization applies to all organizations, both formal and informal.

Like the need for a heartbeat, the need for a reliable bond is basic, primitive, inborn, and universal. Consequently, any act that threatens or terminates that bond creates debilitating illness, both physical and mental. A breaking of that bond results in the anaclitic depression and marasmus (wasting away) discussed elsewhere in this book. As James Lynch asserts in *The Broken Heart: The Medical Consequences of Loneliness*, separation and the feeling of loneliness it engenders are a major cause of premature death from heart disease and a contributing factor to many other life-threatening illnesses.[46] Loneliness and separation not only hurt, they also kill. Apparently, the devastating impact of the broken heart is more than a figment of the poet's imagination.

All of us have experienced arguments, broken romances, the loss of friends, divorces, deaths in the family, moves from one city to another, and RIFs. Each of us knows the kind of pain and turmoil such separation produces; and knowing that, we are deeply afraid of it and will do almost anything to avoid it. In my opinion, it was that in-born fear of separation and the reciprocal desire for attachment that led Adolph Eichmann to carry out orders with which he might not have agreed. It was his way of attempting to maintain the attachment and support of his superiors, colleagues, and subordinates. He was ter-rified of loneliness; Arendt herself describes him as a man for whom "the official date of Germany's defeat . . . was significant . . . mainly because it dawned upon him that henceforward he would have to live without being a member of something or other."[47]

The same fear of separation and desire for attachment led members of the Jewish councils to collude with their persecutors. Like Eichmann, they feared being detached from the broader German culture of which they were a part and to which they looked for sup-port and attachment. For instance, in 1935, when German Jews were confronted with a hoard of anti-Semitic laws, a prominent member of the Jewish community expressed his fear of separation and desire for attachment when he stated his rationale for colluding with such laws: "Life is possible under every law. . . . A useful and respected citizen can also be a member of a minority in the midst of a great people."[48] In another form, Kren and Rappoport report that the fear of separa-tion and desire for attachment were expressed by members of the Jewish community who could not believe the enormity of the crimes that were being committed against them and the extent to which they were being separated, both metaphorically and literally, from their countrymen: "It cannot be true—such things don't happen."[49] Then, when "such things" did begin to happen, that fear of separation led many Jews to opt to die in the presence of members of their faith rather than to endure the pain of separation that escape from their community would require. As Kren and Rappoport describe a family marched along in the sun. It was easier to die among many than to fight and suffer alone."[50] (Arendt also provides evidence that successful escape was more likely among Jews for whom the sense of community was weak.)[51]

Expressed in a different setting, that same fear of separation and desire for attachment led the university senator to seek his colleagues' separation from the faculty as a means of fulfilling his own needs for attachment with those who remained. ("If you help us get rid of others, my job will be protected and so will yours.") The senator apparently failed to realize that once an organization member becomes expendable, no one, including himself, could ever be secure. All that could be debated was the price that he and others would pay for remaining.

Fear of separation and the desire for attachment caused my colleague to consider the proposal seriously, because—like Eichmann— he would rather be attached than separated. Fortunately, he realized that the most devastating isolation would come from having to live, day to day, with others who would clearly desert (separate) him (or one another) if their own short-term interests were served by that act of organizational genocide. Living with shipmates who would toss you to the sharks when the rations run low is never a comfortable existence. It simply does not build the sense of community, loyalty, and trust that is necessary to ensure the long-term survival of the crew.

Possible Remedies

Knowing that fear of separation and desire for attachment is universal and that no one—not Eichmann, you, or I—is immune from its influence, I have reached what for me is a terrifying conclusion: When Eichmann is in the organization, it is because we are in Eichmann and he is acting on our behalf.

How can we disengage Eichmann's services? We can do that by enshrining the principle that each of us has the right to live in a society (or organization) that affirms our desire to survive. From the foregoing, it would seem that survival requires attachment. Thus, we must build organizations that guarantee employment and garner reciprocal employee obligation. Further, we need to broaden the role of all organization members in formulating policy. We must install structures of altruism in our organizations. Finally, we need to study the Danes and explore moral issues as a part of daily organizational life. Although I think these ideas are germane during times when material resources are limited, I think they have equal relevance during times of material prosperity.

Guaranteed Employment.   If you want to reduce fear of separation and provide a means for meeting the desire for attachment in organizations, guarantee employment. It is not by chance that the Japanese, who guarantee employment to a large portion of their work force, tend to outproduce us in virtually all competitive fields they choose to enter.[52] Assuming that the experience of separation leads to anaclitic depression and marasmus, I think it is reasonable to assume that the Japanese policy of guaranteed employment is an important element of their industrial success. I think it is also reasonable to assume that our failure to guarantee employment and our coincident proclivity to threaten our work force with anaclitic depression and marasmus has much to do with our current economic and spiritual depression.

If organizations guarantee employment, however, employees must reciprocate by committing themselves to long-term employment with their organizations. Obligations must be reciprocal, because when we leave an organization, either voluntarily or involuntarily, we create anaclitic depression and marasmus for those who remain.

An example of such reciprocity is found in Japan. A significant portion of the work force is guaranteed lifetime employment, yet the trade-off is that those workers cannot quit one organization and move to another without serious negative consequence. In fact, if they do quit, they are virtually excluded from future employment opportunities with high-status organizations.

Since job-hopping has long been sanctioned in our culture, I suspect that the requirement that we obligate ourselves to our organizations (that is, to one another) will be very difficult for most of us to accept. As Philip Slater has indicated in the *Pursuit of Loneliness: American*

Culture at the Breaking Point, we have unconsciously adopted a pattern of thought based on the belief that each of us can live in lonely independence from one another.[53] That pattern, in turn, causes us to pursue marasmic separation ("I'm not going to be tied down to a job, spouse, friends, organization, or location") while starving for life-giving attachment to others. Given the entrenched nature of that thought pattern, it will require a lot of discipline and energy to change it.

The concept of guaranteed employment and reciprocal obligation also may be difficult to accept because they create an organization in which moral obligation is an important aspect of organizational life. Akio Morita, who built the Sony Corporation, implicitly spoke of that moral obligation when he said that "a company is a fate-sharing body."[54] If we accept that premise, each of us must be willing to follow the lead of the Danes and put on the "yellow arm band" when *any* member of our organization is threatened with "extermination." Those of us who have been trained to think as amoral pragmatists may find that such moral obligations demand more of us than we can easily offer.

The list of changes that would be required is virtually endless. However, it might include:

1. Taking more care in hiring new people
2. Placing greater emphasis on long-range planning
3. Motivating one another by appealing to our needs for attachment rather than to our pathological fears of separation
4. Designing compensation and incentive systems that reward interdependent teamwork rather than cutthroat internecine competition
5. Compensating organization members more equitably. (It is not by chance that the real after-tax income of CEOs of major Japanese firms is six to seven times that of a newly hired college graduate, whereas in American corporations, the ratio can easily exceed fifty to one.)[55]
6. Fostering a climate of cooperation, rather than adversarial rela-

tionships, between groups such as labor and management. (When that happens, Johnny Paycheck will no longer serenade country music fans with songs such as "Take This Job and Shove It.")[56]

Participative Management. The right to participate in the control of change constitutes another approach to reducing the fear of separation that leads to evil. It also provides the opportunity to experience the attachment that is required for love and, therefore, is particularly germane when organizations are under economic pressures that might otherwise result in RIFs.

Elliott Jaques defines participation as "the right of employees to collectively take part in the control of any changes whatever which they feel might adversely affect their future employment opportunities as a group." He continues: "Participation is thus intimately associated with belongingness and alienation. For a person to have a sense of belongingness requires the opportunity to belong."[57]

Externally imposed changes that might adversely affect one's own employment create separation, anaclitic depression, and marasmus. Since fear of separation is universal, few people—especially healthy ones—ever willingly cooperate with changes that might cause them to feel separated, particularly with changes that might cost them their employment.

Consequently, participation, or what is frequently termed "participative management," is effective only when it includes the right of *all* individuals to protect their needs for attachment. As Jaques argues, if employees are to participate, the managerial prerogative to limit participation cannot exist. Abridged participation is reminiscent of the activities of the Jewish council members, who could decide only the order in which the trains to Auschwitz would be loaded. Those limited participants in the management process could not decide whether the trains *would* be loaded.

Participation also eliminates resistance to change as a rationale for inhumane organizational behavior. *Resistance to change* is a behavioral science term frequently used by those whose sense of attachment is not threatened to rationalize taking the inhumane action of creating anaclitic depression: "We have to do something about those people who are resisting the introduction of robots. Sure, they will lose their jobs once the robots are in place, but that's the way life is. They are resistant to change, but they can't block progress."

Structures of Altruism. A third way in which organizations could facilitate love and reduce alienation is to create organizational policies and procedures that encourage members to express altruism. Again, the opportunity to express altruism is particularly important when material resources are limited.

Altruism, according to sociobiologist Edmund Wilson, is "generosity without hope of reciprocation," is genetic in origin, and is a necessary condition for the survival of the species.[58] Vaillant describes altruism as "getting pleasure from giving to others what you yourself would like to receive," and he considers it one of the mature adaptations to life.[59]

However it is defined, altruism is a source of attachment, growth, and pleasure to those who give and receive it. In contrast, firing, cutting, axing, and terminating others are not expressions of altruism. They are expressions of greed. They produce alienation and separation. They prepare us to commit holocaust.

Why is altruism so seldom encouraged by formal organizations? Perhaps, as both Vaillant and Wilson assert, altruism is not widely distributed in the culture. Because organizations seldom condone altruism, it would not be surprising if that quality were relatively rare. Nevertheless, I disagree with Vaillant and Wilson; I believe that we have a deep desire to express altruism.

For instance, when faced with a potential RIF, 87 percent of 1,400 employees surveyed by the Census Bureau in Suitland, Maryland, said that they would rather take up to sixteen days of furlough in lieu of an RIF. The *Fairfax Journal* speculated about the Suitland employees: "The people here are willing to share the burden. They'd rather take more furlough days than have someone lose their job."[60] In a similar fashion, A&P grocery store employees in parts of Virginia voted two to one in favor of significant pay cuts rather than seeing coworkers lose their jobs.[61] Although self-interest might have been involved for some, those whose jobs presently were secure clearly chose altruism when they opted for "give-backs" over co-worker misery. The frequency of similar generosity in the workplace indicates to me that the desire to express altruism is widely distributed. Organizations just lack structures through which it can be easily expressed.

Someday, though, structures and procedures that encourage the expression of altruism will be commonplace. Responding to our collective needs for attachment and survival, we will invent routine procedures that will formalize our desires to be decent and kind in the presence of those with whom we work. Referenda of the type conducted by the Census Bureau will be required and commonplace. Discussing approaches for legitimizing expressions of organizational altruism, a president of a small company asked me, "Assuming my people are altruistic and want to save others' jobs, how do I find that out?"

My reply was, "Ask them."

He first said, "That never occurred to me." Then, after some period of thought, he asked, "What if I find they are altruistic? Then am I required to follow the altruistic policies their answer implies? Wouldn't I be giving up my prerogatives to manage my business as I see fit?" To me, he seems to be asking the correct question.

Learning from the Danes. My final suggestion for making organizations humane is that we be willing to learn from the Danes. For instance, we need to know why the Danes were able to take their fear of separation and need for attachment and, rather than providing fuel for the ovens of Auschwitz, turn their needs into acts of survival and love. I have always wondered why we know so little about them.

Arendt, for instance, devotes only five pages of her work to the Danes' extraordinary expression of love. Rather than exploring it in depth, she refers to it as a "sui generis" event.[62] Then she devotes approximately 290 pages to various descriptions of the atrocities.

I don't know of a single, well-known book that discusses the Danes' act of courageous love in depth or in detail. Perhaps such books exist, but to my knowledge, none has received the attention that books on the Holocaust have received.

Although I am depressed about how little we know about the Danes, I am impressed with how much we know about the Japanese and their approach to work. In the service of our apparently insatiable curiosity, authors have inundated us with books such as *Theory Z*,[63] *The Art of Japanese Management*,[64] and *For Harmony and Strength*.[65] I contend, though, that the Japanese approach to organization is one for which the time has come, just as our North American approach to organization is one for which the time has passed. The Danes, on the other hand, expressed an approach to organization for which the time has neither come nor passed. I suspect that their approach is timeless, and for that reason, it demands timeless study.

If the Danes' contribution is so important, why have we ignored it? For me, the answer to that question is simple. For us to clearly understand what led the Danes to take enormous risks by refusing to collude in the murder of their own people, some of whom happened to be Jews, we have to be willing to take the same enormous risks in our daily organizational lives. In addition, such understanding will inevitably lead us into the exploration of moral, ethical, and spiritual issues of organizational life. For most of us, such exploration is not easy or comfortable, because it deals with the essence of our respective souls. At the same time, the willingness to deal with the ethical, the moral, and the spiritual is the most important requirement for creating effective organizations.

Learning to make conscious, thoughtful, moral choices in dealing with small organizational matters is the way we prepare ourselves to make moral choices when the big issues are involved. As I said earlier, it is particularly heroic to take moral stands when the stakes are apparently low, because the implications of our choices are not as apparent to us and to others. Whatever the stakes, it clearly is not easy to make organizational choices that are moral, ethical, and spiritual. Moral choices are always acts of will that express our affectionate concern for others. They are expressions of our desire to ensure that we and others survive. They are expressions of courage.

In that light, perhaps the vanished hippies of the sixties were unwitting allies of future generations of executives when they said, "It takes courage to make love, not war."

Amen.

7

Group Tyranny and the Gunsmoke Phenomenon

B ECAUSE we worship individuality, we apparently need to believe that groups are tyrannical and that an individual's intellectual and moral integrity are inherently in conflict with irrational, tyrannical pressures to conform. In the service of that need, we have co-opted social scientists to produce theories and research that support that view. In *Totem and Taboo*, Sigmund Freud attempted to demonstrate how the dynamics of primitive group tyranny destructively coerce individuals to act contrary to deeply held beliefs and values.[1] Experiments by Solomon Asch suggest that individuals will conform even when faced with obvious contradictory perceptual information.[2] Bion's notion of unconscious group mental states[3] and Janis's theories regarding groupthink[4] also bolster the idea that group tyranny forces individuals to violate their own precepts. Being a true believer in the basic underlying theory, I even added my doctoral dissertation to the chorus singing praises to peer pressure, group conformity, and group tyranny.[5]

I have now become convinced that group tyranny seldom occurs. Rather, for the most part, it is a culturally sanctioned negative fantasy, designed by behavioral scientists and management theorists to provide us with an excuse for blaming someone else when we lose our sense of integrity and act irresponsibly in group situations. I reached that conclusion in two ways.

First, I observed a phenomenon I call the Abilene Paradox (see chapter 2). Briefly I concluded that the dynamics of action anxiety, negative fantasies, real existential risk, fear of separation, and the reversal of risk and certainty frequently lead groups to take collective actions contrary to the desires of any of their individual members. In writing my essay on the Abilene Paradox, it occurred to me that what we traditionally call conformity behavior could frequently be a trip to Abilene. That is, all participants could feel pressured into a course of action that none of them wanted to take as individuals, but each could attribute his or her individual behavior to being coerced by a group, even though such coercion didn't exist.

Second, I reread a number of psychological experiments that ostensibly demonstrate the dynamics of group tyranny and conformity pressures. Reading in the light of the Abilene Paradox, I have found that in virtually none of the studies are individuals actually pressured by groups to conform to anything. One such example is the classic Asch experiment that serves as the prototypical psychological study demonstrating the negative impact of group pressure on individual behavior.[6]

As some readers will recall from Asch's well-publicized research, seven people were invited to participate in what was presumably a perception study. They sat in a row, facing the experimenter, who explained that their task was very simple. They were to look at twelve sets of cards, two at a time (see figure 7–1). The participants in the experiment were instructed to report which of the comparison lines was equal in length to the standard line. As you can tell, their task was simple at face value, because the required judgments are so obvious that one would have to be nearly blind to make a mistake.

I say "at face value" because, unknown to one naive participant (called "the critical subject"), the other six participants were confederates who were secretly cooperating with the experimenter. The confederates had received instructions on how to respond to each set of cards. In addition, the naive person was maneuvered to be one of the last people to express the perceptual judgment. Thus, the critical subject replied after hearing the responses of most of the others.

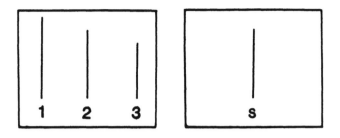

Comparison Lines   **Standard Line**

Figure 7-1. SAMPLE TASK FOR THE ASCH EXPERIMENT

Approximately half of the time the shills (euphemistically called "instructed subjects") were told to give the correct answer: "The standard line equals line two." Unknown to the naive critical subject, the other half of the time the shills were instructed to give a unanimously incorrect answer—for example, "The standard line equals line one." Consequently, the naive subject was suddenly confronted with a discrepancy between the information reaching his eyeballs and that reaching his eardrums. His eyeballs told him that the standard line was the same length as line two, but the other participants had said, "S equals one." Does he vote according to his eyeballs or his eardrums?

Well, approximately one-third of the critical subjects who participated in the study went with their eardrums, contradicting the obviously correct visual judgment by saying, "S equals one." Furthermore, their willingness to give an incorrect answer under those conditions has been described by Asch and many others as a scientific demonstration of the generic process by which individuals give up their intellectual and emotional integrity and capitulate to group pressure.

Yet if you carefully read the Asch experiment—and many others that have been modeled after it—you will discover that no pressure was exerted by members of the instructed group. The six confederates didn't intimidate, cajole, ridicule, ostracize, demean, threaten, belittle or in any other way coerce the naive participant. In short, they exerted no pressure. Rather, they preyed upon the naive subject's fear of separation, a fear that stems from people's instinctive, existential desire to avoid the ravages of anaclitic depression and marasmus. However, these manifestations of internal, inborn fears have frequently been described as examples of the ways in which groups exert external pressure on recalcitrant members to conform.

Outside the laboratory, the erroneous interpretation of the experiment has been used to explain everything from the impact of peer pressure on teenage delinquency ("They are basically good kids; they just robbed the bank because of peer pressure") to the U.S. disaster at the Bay of Pigs. In the latter example, key policymakers allegedly were pressured by other group members into taking a course of action contrary to their true beliefs.[7]

Why do we consistently blame such actions on conformity pressures, when the behavior is probably attributable to our fear of separation? Perhaps the culturally sanctioned negative fantasy of group tyranny relieves us of responsibility for our own actions. Thus, it temporarily frees us from experiencing the terrifying existential risk of separation.

In more practical terms, so long as we can convince ourselves and others that the sinister forces of groupthink prevented us from confronting a controversial issue during a staff meeting or that peer pressure caused our juvenile delinquency, we don't have to accept responsibility for our own behaviors. In fact, we can blame others for all our mortal sins and minor peccadilloes. However, we may be nervous about our absolution, because we know that the fantasy of group pressure doesn't ring quite true.

Belief in the inherent conflict between individuality and conformity pressures may provide us with a Garden of Eden. The centerpiece of this Eden is a tree of knowledge whose apples grow well above our reach. So long as we are not faced with the opportunity of tasting the knowledge such fruit provides, we are not confronted with significant moral choices—choices that are the essence of spiritual experience in all kinds of organizations.

The Gunsmoke Phenomenon as a Useful Myth

Most people don't read the group tyranny theories of Freud, Bion, or Asch. How, then, has the fantasy that the behavior of individuals is inevitably in conflict with the irrational demands of tyrannical groups managed to permeate our ethos?

In the United States—and perhaps generally in Western civilization—I think that belief is acquired by observing the dynamics of what I call the Gunsmoke phenomenon. Novels, movies, and television and radio dramas have exposed millions of people to the myth of the individual in conflict with group tyranny. Beginning at a very young age, we repeatedly are exposed to the message that we must surrender our intellectual and moral integrity in order to survive in a world that requires that we conform to the tyranny of groups.

Here is how the Gunsmoke phenomenon works: At least twice a year, some TV program recapitulates an archetypal "Gunsmoke" plot, in which a poor dirt farmer is riding across the prairie to Dodge City to get provisions for his pregnant wife and their ten bedraggled kids. Eight miles outside of town on a little-used trail, his horse steps into a gopher hole and goes lame. At the same time, the Frickert Gang is robbing the Dodge City Bank. In the process, they murder the teller and steal half the horses in the town to thwart the posse. The varmints escape by the same trail on which the expectant father is waiting forlornly for help. Being greedy, Jesse Frickert, the gang's leader, sells the farmer a stolen horse, which the farmer innocently rides to Dodge City.

Immediately upon arrival, the farmer is arrested by Marshal Dillon. The marshal charges him with horse theft, murder, and bank robbery, which—as you probably know—are not misdemeanors. Dillon always throws the poor fellow in jail, but from his cell the guy stoutly contends that he is blameless. Dillon always tends to believe him. Saying that he has heard that the man has a good reputation in the county, the marshal speculates that a jury probably will find him innocent.

Unfortunately, though, the judge is out of town. (He always seems to be in Pecos at a convention, and it always seems to take him a minimum of five days to ride back to conduct the trial.) So Dillon explains that the man will have to wait in jail until the judge returns to release him. "Assuming that you are innocent," Dillon says, "and I believe that you probably are, the jury will acquit you, and we will get Doc Adams out in time to tend to the missus and to deliver number eleven. I'm going to have to lock you up until then, but don't worry. This is a fair, law-abiding town, and assuming that you ain't lying, everything's going to turn out all right."

Then night comes, and you know as well as I what happens. A mob forms at the local saloon—in this case, the Longbranch. Someone shouts, "Let's hang him. Ain't no need for waiting for no dumb circuit judge to get back from carousing around in Pecos. We caught him dead to rights, so let's string him up, get it over with, and get this town back on an even keel."

And just as suddenly, everyone breaks for their ropes. There is always a tearful scene played out somewhere as one member of the potential mob gallops up to his house on his trusty steed. He suddenly pulls up the reins, his horse plants its haunches, and he begins to dismount as they slide to the hitching post in a cloud of dust. The rider whips the reins around the post, runs into the house, and shouts to his sleepy wife, who—though just aroused from a deep slumber—is always starched and prim in her nightgown: "Lou Ann, whar's my rope?"

"What do you want a rope for, Sam? Have the cattle broke out?"

"Woman, just help me find my rope and don't ask no questions!"

"But Sam, I don't understand why you need a rope in the middle of the night. Are the horses loose?"

"The horses ain't loose, but your jaw's going to be loose if you don't quit your yammering. Just shut up and help me find my rope."

And then it dawns on her what is really happening. "Oh, Sam," she says as she grabs hold of him, "you ain't a-gonna hang him, are you? Oh, please don't. It ain't fair. He deserves a fair trial. Think of our kids, Sam. How can you ever look 'em in the eye if you do it? Please don't—for my sake. Oh God, Sam, I'm begging you . . . please."

But before she can finish her sentence, Sam pushes her away and grabs the rope, which has been in plain view all along. As he mounts his horse and rides toward the open prairie, he mumbles to her in a half-incomprehensible voice, "I don't want to do it, but everyone else does."

After essentially the same scene is played out at various locations in the area, a mob assembles at the Longbranch and begins what is called the "torchlight parade" up Main Street. They head toward the jail, which also doubles as the marshal's office.

Dillon, vaguely aware that something is amiss, is always squinting around the shutter that covers the front window. As it dawns on him what is happening, he turns to Festus, his chief confidant and the equivalent of the administrative assistant in contemporary organizations. Dillon shouts, "Festus, a mob is heading this way from the Longbranch. Take a shotgun, stand by the cell, and try to hold 'em off if they get through the front door. I'll go out and see if I can cool 'em off."

At this moment, we, the viewers of this mythological event portrayed on our TV, are saying, "Look at that. A riot. One solitary man aligned in lonely conflict against the tyrannical forces of an irrational mob. It reminds me of what goes on at my office. Can Dillon hold out?"

The question seems legitimate enough. Unknown to us, though, as we interpret the conflict as individuality versus mob rule, we are subtly training ourselves and others to believe in the negative fantasy of group tyranny. In turn, the more we believe that fantasy, the more likely we are to use conformity pressures as excuses for failing to act with courageous integrity in other organizational settings.

Then, as we take another bite from the wormy apple of the Tree of False Knowledge, Marshal Dillon steps out the door of the jail. I'm always amazed at what happens.

Five hundred burly men are assembled in the street. They have wagons, pistols, shotguns, rifles, torches, ropes, knives, signs, whiskey, horses, mules, telegraph poles, sledgehammers, and horsewhips. In addition, small boys are peering from beneath every porch and doorstep in the vicinity. Likewise, women of all ages are peeking between the curtains from every candle-lit room that fronts on the main street of town.

Despite the chaos and scrutiny, Dillon steps forward and—in a calm, nonchalant, nearly insouciant voice—says, "Howdy."

Someone in the crowd always replies, "Howdy, Marshal. Nice night, ain't it?" (This is called the "introductory palaver"; it is a necessary prelude for the second phase of the ritual encounter, which afficionados term "the escalation.")

"Marshal, you know why we are here."

"I know why you're here," Dillon replies, "but there ain't gonna be any hanging tonight. This star [as he taps the gilded badge that glitters above his left shirt pocket] says everybody in this town gets a fair chance. So get back to the Longbranch, to your drinking and card-playing and women. You'll get your day in court."

And once again we viewers say, "What tyranny! What conflict! What conformity pressures! One solitary man standing alone against a crazed mob. Peer pressure at its worst. Can Dillon hold out?"

Then someone shouts, "We ain't here to hassle you, Marshal, but we're a-gonna hang him."

Dillon replies, "And I'm not here to hassle you, either, but nobody's coming in this jail."

To which an unshaven man wearing a dusty black hat responds, "If that's the way you want it, that's the way you're a-gonna get it. Step aside, Marshal, 'cause here we come."

The mob surges forward and we tube-viewers say, "Dillion is in real trouble. They are going to get him for sure."

But after three steps, the deep voice of our beloved marshal booms forth: "Hold it right where you are. You see this line on the ground, fellows?" And he scratches a line about four feet long with the heel of his boot.

"We see it, Marshal."

"First person to step across it gets his head blown off."

There is a lengthy silence, and then someone in the crowd says, "Well, if you put it that way," and the crowd slowly disappears.

At the same time, we couch potatoes say to one another, "What a hero! One individual, aligned in lonely conflict against the primitive forces of group tyranny and mob rule, faced them eyeball-to-eyeball and they blinked. What courage!"

Dillon did exhibit courage, but not in the face of conformity pressures, because those forces were no more present in this situation than they were in the Asch experiment. His courage came from running the risk of helping the people in the mob do exactly what they wanted to do from the start—to extricate themselves from the situation without too much loss of face. In metaphorical terms, he helped avert a trip to Abilene, because the townsfolk didn't really want to hang anyone. In addition, as a marshal, he didn't want to let the prisoner be hanged, for reasons of both justice and practicality. Just imagine the reports, red tape, and paperwork that a lynching might cause. And the potential hangee would be against it, I suspect, for a variety of reasons.

The wormy apple we eat has always led us to describe the situation in terms of mob rule and peer pressure. Why? Again, I answer that interpreting the situation in terms of conflict and tyranny rather than agreement and cooperation exempts us from taking the same enormous risk Dillon took as we deal with our families, our colleagues, our friends, and other organizations.

In other words, like Adam and Eve, we do not want to partake of a fresh apple from the Tree of Knowledge, particularly an apple that suggests that group tyranny seldom exists. We fear the knowledge that groups generally offer a tremendous amount of support and freedom, if only we choose to accept it when it is offered. That is why we shout, "Please, Marshal Dillon, don't shoot a new apple from the upper reaches of the Tree of Knowledge." We shout it because the apple's availability will confront us with a difficult and risky set of moral choices—choices many of us would prefer to avoid.

For instance, once we have partaken of the new apple, the easy excuse, "My peers pressured me into doing it," will not be available to the teenager who is caught stealing from the variety store. The groupthink alibi will not be available to the executive who is asked, "Why don't you say what you really believe in the staff meeting?" The mob rule explanation will not suffice when a military bureaucrat receives the query, "Why did you participate in the extermination of Jews?" In fact, because we need easy excuses, we probably will continue to encourage and subsidize social scientists, novelists, and scriptwriters to provide us with variations of mind-numbing, morally anesthetizing apples. We want the apples that produce single-minded devotion to the belief in fantasized conformity pressures, group tyranny, and mob rule.

Eating those wormy apples will deter Marshal Dillon from shooting a different, more demanding apple from the tree. The knowledge provided by the new apple might require that we take the same enormous risk that Dillon took—the risk of existential separation, the ultimate separation being death. And in the absence of faith in divine support, that risk may be too great for many of us to bear.

Existential Risk

If group tyranny is an overrated notion, is Marshal Dillon any less courageous? Is facing down separation anxiety a less courageous act than bucking the angry mob's pressure to conform?

Let's watch "Gunsmoke" a week later to consider another scenario: Once more, a man is riding toward Dodge City to get provisions for his pregnant wife and ten kids. At the identical location, eight miles out on the trail, his horse steps into the same gopher hole and goes lame.

The Frickert Gang strikes again, murders the new teller, and steals most of the remaining horses in town to thwart the posse. Once again, they ride out of town on the same trail, meet the new victim, and sell him a stolen horse, which he, in turn, naively rides into Dodge City.

Dillon, true to the Marshals' Code, arrests him, throws him in jail, and announces that the judge has returned to Pecos to attend some more meetings of the Benevolent Judges' Association but that, come Friday, the new man will get his stint before the bar of justice, after which Dillon and Kitty will get Doc Adams out to deliver number eleven.

Night comes, the mob forms at the Longbranch, and Dillon looks out the right-hand side of the shutter and shouts to his administrative assistant, "Festus, we have another agreement management situation festering at the Longbranch. Take the symbolic shotgun, sit by the cell, and I'll go out, make the usual speech, and break this thing up. Then you and me and Kitty will go have a beer."

"Howdy, Marshal."

"Howdy, fellows. Nice seeing you again."

"You know why we're here."

"I know why you're here, but you might as well get back to the Longbranch."

"Marshal, we don't want to hassle with you."

"And I don't want to hassle with you either, so get back to the Longbranch."

"Marshal, this time we're a-coming in."

"No, you're not."

"Yes we are."

"And this badge says you aren't."

"Marshal, we've told you once. We've told you twice. We ain't gonna tell you a third time. We're coming in over or around you or through you."

"And I've told you once. I've told you twice. I'm not going to tell you a third time. Nobody is coming in this jail."

Then Billy Bob—a gun-waving, one-eyed, mustachioed miscreant—shouts, "Step aside, Marshal, here we come."

Dillon yells, "Hold it! See this line on the ground, fellows?" And in his easy, unaffected way he traces it anew with the heel of his well-worn boot.

"We see it, Marshal."

"First man to step across . . . "—and as he reaches that point of his soliloquy, he gasps as a bullet hole the size of a pie plate appears in his stomach.

As he crumples to the ground and Miss Kitty rushes to his side, he looks up and says, "I misperceived the existential risk."

Apparently separation—including the ultimate separation, death—is an existential risk. A Marshal Dillon devoid of the myth of group tyranny is still courageous to face the existential risk that affiliation, justice, good sense, and love are more characteristic of any given group than alienation, injustice, irrationality, and hate. Before making his moral and sensible stand, Marshal Dillon can only estimate how likely it is that a bullet from Billy Bob Daniel's .44 will make a ventilation hole above the Marshal's navel.

If you cannot accept the possibility of the bullet in the stomach that real tyranny offers, then you must live under the debilitating constraints inherent in the fantasy of group tyranny. Alternatively, if you can accept the possibility of a sizable gunshot wound slightly above your belly button—an event that always involves some form of separation—then you also may experience the existential liberation that community, engagement, and attachment with others provides. Or as Leon Salzman so poetically described, "To be happy, one must risk unhappiness; to live fully, one must risk death and accept its ultimate decision."[8]

For many of us, it is far better that our mythical marshal behave as though he is inevitably in lonely, alienated conflict with the forces of group tyranny. So long as we see him at the mercy of a capricious mob, he leaves the apple that requires existential risk and moral choice in the upper reaches of the Tree of Knowledge. Robbed of the richness of choice provided by that apple, we can curse the tyrannical Devil of Conformity Pressures and Mob Rule. We need that devil. Otherwise, we may discover the enormous potential for the development of our souls—a development that always involves the risk of connection with and commitment to a relationship of vulnerability to others.

Making the Choice

A belief in the new myth of the courageous marshal who accepts the existential risk involves the realization that we have a choice when confronted with the possibility of group tyranny. Given that choice and the risk that accompanies it, I have found that answering a few questions can help people in organizations decide which choice they wish to make.

The first question is, "What action would you really like to take?" When managers and other organization members arrive at unedited, spontaneous answers to that question, they often describe an action that is ultimately sensible. Marshal Dillon might answer, "Draw a line on the ground and threaten to dispatch the head from the shoulders of the first person who crosses it." The union leader might respond, "Recommend to the membership that we offer management of the distressed company the option of shorter hours with no layoffs or a full-on strike if they attempt to unfairly dismiss a few of the least senior employees."

Logically, the second question is, "What keeps you from taking such action?" That question is designed to ascertain the negative fantasies that prevent you from doing what you believe to be sensible. When working with managers on real-life problems, I have collected up to eight single-spaced, typewritten pages of fantasized disasters that individuals believe might befall them if they behave in a manner they believe to be sensible.

Next, a decision maker might reasonably be asked what the *best* and *worst* possible outcomes would be if the desired solution were attempted. The same questions can be asked about failing to take the desired action. The crucial question, of course, is, "How probable is each of those four possible outcomes?" When I have later been able independently to discover the true probabilities, I have found that most people had come very close to predicting the actual odds.

For example, some time ago I interviewed a man who worked for the U.S. Government and wanted to try something risky and innovative. He was afraid to try his plan, though, "because there is a lot of pressure to conform around here and to do things the way they have always been done. If I try anything new, I may get fired."

"What's the probability of your actually getting fired?" I asked.

"Oh, 50 percent, I would say."

I pressed, "Do you really believe that the probability of getting fired is 50 percent?"

"No, of course not. It's more like one in a million."

Since the federal Civil Service Commission reported that in 1977, only 200 out of a nonmilitary work force of 2.5 million were fired for failing to do their work properly,[9] his second estimate was much closer, at least for practical purposes, than the first. In addition, if you inquire why another 18,800 were fired from the federal government during the same year, you will find that they had to do something like sodomize a horse in the lobby of a public building during working hours in the presence of three corroborating witnesses—twice. In short, the probability of getting fired because of resisting conformity pressures was essentially zero—not 50 percent, as the respondent initially contended.

If you can't accept the possibility of the worst that could happen if you behave sensibly, regardless of how small that possibility may be, then you have to suffer the ravages of group tyranny. Paradoxically, you have to suffer them even if such tyranny is only mythical. Or, in the Gunsmoke metaphor, if you can t accept the risk of a bullet in the stomach, you have to open the jail door, collude with the mob in sacrificing an innocent victim, blame your actions on group tyranny, and hope that the grand jury interpret the Asch experiment to mean that conformity is caused by irresistible group pressure.

I ask decision makers, "What support do you need from others to take the sensible and moral action?" I assume that no one can take a risky action without the emotional support of someone else. Separation anxiety, anaclitic depression, and marasmus are existential conditions of life, and even heroic marshals are not immune to their influence. The independent, stoic western sheriff portrayed by John Wayne exists only in our imagination. All the Marshal Dillons of this world have a source of connection and support—perhaps unseen—that provides them with the courage to take the existential risk of separation. Even the *Lone* Ranger had the support of his faithful Indian companion, Tonto.

The final question for the decision maker to answer is, "What action do you plan to take?" This question assumes that any action—including *no* action—in the face of possible group tyranny has a risk. Nothing in life is totally predictable, and about all we can do is live within the limits of our best reality-bound predictions of the world around us and then accept what happens. Or as Damon Runyan reportedly paraphrased some lines from Ecclesiastes: "The race may not go to the swift, nor the battle to the strong, but that's the way to bet 'em."

This approach to coping leaves one feeling bleak, though, if it represents only a probability statement of rewards and punishments in a universal crapshoot. Well, then, what is the ultimate purpose of determining whether the forces of group tyranny are real or fantasized?

For me, the question again becomes one of spiritual transcendence. More specifically, can one transcend the world of secular probabilities in a manner that provides spiritual meaning to the process of coping with what we heretofore have called peer pressure, conformity dynamics, and group tyranny? More important, can one cope with the alternatives that involve liberation and freedom?

We answer those questions by deciding how to deal with the threat of separation that underlies what we erroneously term group tyranny. Thus, the answers are ultimately in the realm of the religious, the spiritual, and the theological, rather than the statistical, the sociological, or the psychological. Coping with group tyranny—whether real or fantasized—is always a spiritual matter. This is true whether such coping involves conforming to nonsense in a business meeting, capitulating to peer pressure as a teenager, or standing alone—but not lonely—against a lynch mob.

If one happens to come from a Christian religious tradition, one may find support and courage before the mob by remembering the words of Jesus as he spoke to the disciples after he transcended his encounter with a tyrannical mob (Matthew 28:20): "And lo, I am with you always."

Or if one's spiritual predilection is Jewish, one may find the courage to experience the existential risk from the words of a singing sheriff (Psalms 27:1): "The Lord is my light and my salvation; whom shall I fear? The Lord is the stronghold of my life; of whom shall I be afraid?"

If one's religious tradition comes from the East, the paradoxical wisdom offered by Lao Tsu may provide a meditative marshal with the courage to face the existential reality that is confronting him rather than the fantasy that is not: "Happiness is rooted in misery. Misery lurks beneath happiness. Who knows what the future holds?"

Or finally, if you share "Einstein's Intoxication with the God of the Cosmos,"[10] you may develop your own cosmic view of the divine that provides both meaning to your world and the courage to risk living in it.

In my experience, the tyranny of groups, both real and fantasized, dissolves in the presence of a source of transcendent spiritual support.

8

Encouraging Future Managers to Cheat

A s a management professor, I have long believed that I have an ethical responsibility to encourage the students in my classes to cheat. (For reasons that will become apparent, I feel that responsibility keenly in the case of the students who aspire to roles as managers.) Recently, that belief was enhanced when my son applied for admission to the University of Virginia, an institution that prides itself on its honor system. Reading the application materials, he found: "On all written work done by students at the University of Virginia, the following pledge is either required or implied: 'On my honor as a student, I have neither given nor received aid on this assignment.'" He was also warned that anyone who breaches that pledge commits academic fraud, is in violation of the honor system, and will be expelled from the university.[1] Although other universities may not have formal honor codes, giving and receiving aid on written assignments, particularly examinations, is generally frowned upon and is usually accorded the more commonplace title "cheating." Regardless of the semantics used to describe such nefarious behavior, the penalties for engaging in it tend to be severe.

Does it strike you as odd, though, that virtually all educational institutions in our culture, from kindergarten through graduate school, define cheating as "giving aid to others or receiving aid from them"? More specifically, does it strike you as unusual that we define cheating as an act of helping or being helped by others? Does it seem in any way peculiar to you that an expression of altruism has become an avatar of behavior that is immoral, dishonorable, and sullied? Alternatively, does it not strike you as bizarre that by defining cheating as the process of helping others, we implicitly are saying that *not* being helpful—being narcissistic and selfish—is a prototypical expression of academic decency and honor?

It does me. In fact, I believe that defining cheating in that way is unethical, immoral, and, consequently, educationally unsound—unless, of course, one of our purposes as educators is to provide training in the attitudes and skills required for destroying ourselves and others. When that definition of cheating is imposed upon the future leaders and followers of our business community, we virtually guarantee that our organizations will lack the unity and spirit of teamwork essential to compete in the world economy.

Practical Consequences of Our Definition of Cheating

To define cheating as giving and receiving aid creates a whole range of problems—problems that I know few of us want or intend to create.

It Provides a Lousy Model for How Work Really Gets Done

In his classic study on how managers spend their time, Mintzberg found that typical managers spend about 20 percent of their time working alone.[2] The remaining 80 percent is spent talking with others on the telephone, in face-to-face meetings with other individuals, or in group meetings. Surgeons don't go into the operating room and say to the nurses, aides, and fellow physicians who surround them, "It is against my principles to give or receive aid during surgery." I know of no football player who, as a moral imperative, demands that his teammates leave the field before he agrees to carry the ball. And as my colleague Peter Vaill points out, he has never heard of anyone in any organization, other than academia, being given a job to do with the admonition, "As a matter of honor, don't seek help from anyone or give help to anyone as you do it." (You might be interested to know that when I called Peter to check the accuracy of his quotation, he refused to talk with me about it, asserting that to do so would constitute an unethical act of cheating.)

Most people will agree with the pragmatic observation that the world in which actual work is accomplished requires that we give and receive aid, rather than withholding or rejecting it. Consequently, defining cheating as we do has relevance only for organizations in which accomplishing real work is unimportant and perhaps even actively discouraged.

It Thwarts the Expression of Synergy

Requiring that business students work in lonely isolation from one another also thwarts the expression of synergy and teamwork. It denies what experts in management have long known: that is, when human beings work together, they can produce a piece of work that is superior to the work of individuals toiling alone. It denies the reality of the research on high-performing systems by my colleague Peter Vaill, who observed: "A .350 hitter is not just a .350 hitter, typically, but a .350 hitter in context."[3] Stated differently, most individuals can perform their best only in the context of working with others. In short, our definition of cheating ignores the reality of what we know and what, ostensibly, we ask business students to learn.

I say "ostensibly" because when examination time comes, we say, "Although we have asked you to read the literature on participation, collaboration, teamwork, and synergy, and although we have given you a number of opportunities to experience those dynamics in classroom demonstrations and exercises, we don't want you—or us management teachers—to have the opportunity to really experience it. We just want you to learn about it. We don't want you to actually practice it."

When we do that, the enormous difference between our espoused theories and our actual practices is exposed to view.[4] The fact that we sanction such educational hypocrisy has profound implications, not only for the training of business people but also for the culture at large. I am particularly struck by the cruel irony of the manner in which examinations on the topic of business ethics are conducted, with marasmic enforcers, called proctors, prowling the room to prevent any overt display of individual mental health and altruistic community building. Understanding that irony, I have become acutely aware of the momentous difference between teaching the ethics of organizational behavior and teaching organizational behavior ethically. In my opinion, unless we become aware of and act on our awareness of that difference, the teaching of business ethics will lose its credibility, which, I opine, is its only unique claim to relevance.

It Thwarts the Expression of Altruism

Altruism—which Vaillant tells us is "the constructive and instinctively gratifying service to others,"[5] the process of "getting pleasure from giving to others what you yourself would like to receive."[6]—is one of the most constructive expressions of mental health in an individual. According to Vaillant, it allows us to "integrate reality, interpersonal relationships and private feelings."[7] It "provides a protective filter for the most searing emotions."[8] It allows us to express empathy and sympathy for others. It is a truly elegant adaptation to life.

Viewing the process from a physiological rather than a psychological perspective, stress researcher Hans Selye contends that altruistic egotism—the process of earning the love of one's neighbor—"permits you to express your talents by the most powerful means of maintaining security and peace of mind."[9] Expressed in the synergy of teamwork, such altruism permits the experience of stress to inspire "not only physical endurance and fortitude, but even mental feats."[10]

Sociobiologist Edmund Wilson suggests that altruism, "generosity without hope of reciprocation," is a "transcendental quality that distinguishes human beings from animals," is transmitted from generation to generation genetically, and is a requirement for the survival of any culture.[11]

Once again, it is a matter of no small consequence when educators define cheating as "giving and receiving help on examinations." It is not inconsequential because we are saying, in essence, that it is immoral for students to develop their capacities for expressing altruism, one of the truly healthy adaptations to life. Ultimately, we are saying that to assist in the culture's care and survival is dishonorable and that one of our jobs as educators is to ensure, if possible, that an important skill required for survival is not transmitted to future generations. Thank God that his Department of Genetics is deaf to our mindless babble.

It Causes Anaclitic Depression

Apart from its mundane consequences in the world of work, our definition of cheating causes anaclitic depression—the primitive, universal form of depression that occurs when we are deprived of people to lean on for emotional support. As I have stated before, anaclitic depression leads us to marasmus—that is, a wasting away, both physically and mentally. Spitz, for example, found that infants who were deprived of emotional support became weepy and lethargic, suffered insomnia, refused to eat, and withdrew into themselves. In short, they developed anaclitic depression; and in the absence of intervention by a supportive adult, they went into a state of marasmus—a condition that, at times, resulted in death. Of those who recovered physically, Spitz saw evidence that they suffered permanent emotional damage.[12] Or as Carl Jung might describe it, they received irreparable injuries to their souls.

Anaclitic depression and marasmus also affect adults. In *The Broken Heart: The Medical Consequences of Loneliness,* James Lynch provides persuasive evidence that in our culture, loneliness is a major cause of premature death from heart disease and of a number of other maladies that cause early death.[13] Loneliness, in turn, is the word we adults use to describe our feelings of anaclitic depression. That loneliness, if prolonged, leads to marasmus no less severe in adults than in infants. As I have said before, competent cardiologists believe that the broken heart is more than a figment of the poet's imagination.

Anaclitic depression and marasmus occur not only in individuals but also in organizations and institutions. For example, Philip Slater, in *The Pursuit of Loneliness: American Culture at the Breaking Point,* contends that in a misguided quest to ensure our sense of individuality, we have designed bureaucracies and institutions that thwart our needs for community, engagement and dependence; in doing so, we have brought our culture to the breaking point.[14] Translated into my language, he is saying that we build organizations and institutions that create anaclitic depression and marasmus on a massive scale; by doing so, we are destroying the human fabric required to ensure our culture's survival. The anguish of "corporate life" stems from the competition, loneliness, and alienation that individuals often feel in the midst of a crowd that, ironically, was assembled for the purpose of cooperation.

For me, then, it is not a trivial matter when management professors in particular, or educators in general, define cheating as "giving and receiving help." It is not trivial because, by doing so, we are creating an environment that fosters anaclitic depression and marasmus, thus threatening the survival of individuals, organizations, institutions, and cultures. In addition, we are denying our students and ourselves the opportunity to express one of the highest forms of human decency— altruism.

Realizing the foregoing consequences of the conventional definition of cheating, I had a heart-to-heart conversation about my academic ethics with the dark side of my soul—the part of my psyche that Carl Jung would undoubtedly refer to as my shadow. I report the conversation verbatim:

My Shadow: What is the purpose of all those simulations of managerial incidents, business exercises, and experiential events you use in the classroom? In essence, what do you hope to accomplish using them?

Me: I want to give business students the opportunity to experience the effect of trust, participation, collaboration, teamwork, synergy, and stuff like that.

My Shadow: That "stuff" you describe seems to deal primarily with values. Do you actually think that those values are worthwhile in the 'real world'?

Me: Of course. If I didn't, would I spend so much time and energy trying to help students understand their relevance for the way organizations operate?

My Shadow: Well, if you really believe that those values are important and relevant, do you allow those future leaders and followers to collaborate, cooperate, participate, synergize, or whatever the hell you want to call it on their tests?

Me (rather lamely):	Not on the actual tests. But I strongly encourage them to study together right up to the time of the exam.
My Shadow (smiling sardonically):	Oh. So you back down when the crunch comes and do it like the rest of us. Well, let me tell you what I think. The difference between you and me is that I'm no hypocrite. I believe you have to kick ass and deal one-on-one. I do exactly what I say I believe in. You don't. That kind of hypocrisy must be tough on you and your students.

As my shadow turned on his heel and walked out, I realized that he had shot an arrow into my heel and that my Achilles tendon was bleeding. I also realized that he must have seen in me what I have seen in managers who espouse the glories of collaboration and teamwork in one breath and in the next announce a competitive bonus plan that pits individual salespersons against one another. When I see that hypocrisy in them or me, I tend to feel both angry and sad. On my better days, I can laugh at the ironic foolishness of it all.

A New Definition of Cheating

Hence, we are on shaky ethical and moral grounds anytime we choose to define cheating as giving and receiving aid on any assignment. By doing so, trainers of managerial talent are saying that it is moral and ethical to create anaclitic depression and marasmus, to deny the opportunity to express altruism, to ensure that the competence and elation of synergy cannot be experienced, and to train people to behave in ways that real work is unlikely to be done. We are saying that it is our job to create the dynamics of sickness. Further, in a stroke of Orwellian doublethink, we claim that it is our job to call such sickness "health" and to convince ourselves and others of the efficacy of that euphemism by contending that it is an expression of decency and honor. I don't believe that any of us intend to say and do those things, but for reasons I don't comprehend, we say and do them nevertheless.

Believing that the conventional definition of cheating reflects poorly on the integrity and credibility of educators, I have redefined cheating and express that redefinition in the form of a letter that participants receive the first day of my class. It is designed to fulfill a small part of what I believe to be my moral responsibility as a professor to encourage cheating. The letter goes as follows:

> You may take the examination alone, with another person, or with as many other people as you would like. I frown on cheating. In fact, I go blind with rage if I catch anyone cheating. I define cheating as the failure to assist others on the examination if they request it. . . . You may refer to notes and reference materials during the exam. You may bring friends, relatives or associates to help you. You may also bring equipment, such as typewriters, computers, musical instruments, sewing machines, cookstoves, cameras or any other contrivance which will provide assistance to you in your work. You may not cheat. If possible, have fun. If not, be competently miserable.[15]

Reactions

Operating on the assumption that cheating is the failure to assist others on an examination if they request it has not been easy. Put mildly, I have experienced more than a few problems and gained more than a few important insights from this foray into what my shadow calls "nonhypocritical professing." Student reaction has been one of the sources of insight and problems.

Student Reaction

I have been surprised how frequently students have chosen to work with one another. When I first offered the possibility of collaborating when it counted, I predicted that, at best, 10 percent would take advantage of that opportunity. Although I have not kept precise records over the past five years, I can say without doubt that at least 95 percent of the 350+ students who have taken the course have chosen to work on their examinations with at least one other person. To date, the largest number who have chosen to work together on a single examination is twenty-one. Apparently, students, like most other normal human beings, have a tremendous desire to help and be helped by others. Truly, altruism is distributed widely in the population. All that is needed is the opportunity to express it legitimately.

In what may appear to contradict what I have just said, I am equally impressed by the intensity with which some students have rejected the idea. Although few in number, those who have rejected it have done so with a vengeance. In fact, a short time ago, six students wrote their department chairman requesting that the course I profess be removed from their curriculum. One of the major concerns was that defining cheating as the failure to help others was a violation of everything they had learned during their academic program, a program in which they said they had always been required to work alone.

In the chapter about phrog farms, I pointed out that a fundamental purpose of many contemporary organizations is to turn good people into phrogs. Discussing the tragedy of life in the organizational swamp, I indicated that it is a lonely life on the lily pad and that the ultimate goal of phrogfessing in schools of swamp maintenance is to prepare tadpoles to live in the shadows of the swamp. To me, those six students poignantly demonstrated in their letter that the goals of the phrogfessors had been achieved all too well.

As for the 5 percent who have chosen to work alone, I have had no indication that any have cheated. I am pleased, because I don't know what I would do if someone did. Go blind with rage, I suppose.

Faculty Reaction

In the same way that I was unprepared for the consistency with which students have accepted my idea, I was equally unprepared for the uniformity with which it has been rejected by my colleagues. In fact, with the exception of a few close friends, faculty members have repudiated it. The strength of their repudiation has varied from the passive, benign neglect one would accord the aimless mental wanderings of an eccentric dotard who feeds the birds ("Harv, you are a nice guy, but your idea is for the birds") to the active rejection one would generally reserve for a suspected terrorist who carries a suspicious-looking package aboard one's favorite shuttle flight to New York ("What are you trying to do—infect the brains of our young people with immoral, communistic thoughts? It's your kind of thinking that led to the demise of the Roman Empire").

Considering the intense fear I have experienced while pursuing an idea foreign to my own background and training, I have not been perturbed by the failure of colleagues to accept the definition and try it out. I have been disturbed, though, by the unwillingness of many colleagues to join me in exploring its moral and intellectual foundations and in thinking about its implications. Perhaps this chapter will provide us an opportunity to engage in that kind of thoughtful exploration.

If the reader is interested in doing that, contemplate this one: What do you do when a student approaches you during an examination and says, "Professor, you have said that the failure to help is cheating and that I can seek help from anyone or anywhere. So would you read what I have written and give me some suggestions for improving it?"

The Contrast between Student Desire and Faculty Belief

I have become aware of the marked contrast between the desire of students to provide altruistic assistance to one another and the belief of faculty members that they have an unquestioned obligation—one that I find distasteful—to ensure that students are kept isolated from one another and from the faculty. By pursuing the false belief that they have such an obligation, educators create—unintentionally, I think—destructive depression in both students and themselves. Although the creation may be unintentional, its effect is no less devastating. That monstrous creation is unethical, immoral, destructive, and, in its own way, evil; for I believe that the suppression of altruism in ourselves and others for the purpose of enhancing or maintaining personal power is always an expression of the darkness of our souls.

Most of us see clearly those acts of evil when they occur outside the halls of ivy and are generally quite critical of them. Why do we spare alienating management education the opprobrium we would heap upon managers if they callously disregarded the belongingness needs of their employees?

For instance, during the recent economic recession, the management of the Census Bureau in Suitland, Maryland, summarily rejected an altruistic employee offer to take proportional furlough days rather than losing co-workers to layoffs. Apparently, the top managers believed that the right to fire—to create anaclitic depression and marasmus—was a managerial prerogative that was essential to assure the bureau's efficient operation. Immediately after the RIFs were announced, approximately 200 appeals were filed—appeals that drained the organization of resources that could have been used to do truly productive work. Because of the energy that was wasted as the appeals were processed, the bureau experienced a clear case of organizational marasmus.

I suspect that most organizational behavior professors would agree that the managers who ordered the RIFs under those circumstances were, at best, insensitive or incompetent or, at worst, unethical or immoral. I believe that the reluctance of management faculty to define cheating as the failure to help one another is equally incompetent and immoral and no less debilitating. Stated differently, our decision to define cheating as "giving and receiving help" deprives the 95 percent of students and faculty who want to express altruism of the opportunity to do so and, in addition, produces no less organizational marasmus in our institutions than the census officials did in theirs. I am saddened that academic policymakers have denied one another the marvelous experience of altruistic synergy that would arise if they defined cheating as the failure to assist others on an exam. I am sure, though, that the world's bureaucratic managers are grateful to them for serving as role models who provide subtle legitimacy for their convoluted psychology.

I am also sure that neither the management of the Census Bureau nor business academicians fully realize that the anaclitic depression and marasmus they supply to others is also the anaclitic depression and marasmus they award to themselves. The managers and academicians seldom call it anaclitic depression and marasmus, but they frequently call it burnout, unaware that it emanates from the loneliness they both give and receive.[16]

Someday, I hope that we develop academic policies that offer the community-building support and compassion most of us feel toward ourselves and others. I'm sure that managers of the world's bureaus would appreciate that even more. I have seen very few managers who have received satisfaction from hurting or being hurt by others; so I think they might be particularly pleased if business educators became role models for the legitimate expression of altruism.

Redefining the Purpose of an Examination

Defining cheating as I do has again raised questions for me: "What is the purpose of an examination?" and "What is the meaning of a grade?"

Prior to defining the term, I did not have a satisfactory answer to either question. Now I have a semisatisfactory answer for one—the first: An examination is an opportunity to learn to work in an environment that allows us to solve problems in the best way we can. Thus, an examination is the equivalent of producing a movie and finding out how audiences treat it at the box office, writing a novel and discovering whether anyone sees fit to read it, or creating a product and ascertaining whether anyone in the marketplace wants to buy it. Ultimately, it is an opportunity to learn to use whatever knowledge and skills we have to master a particular problem. As far as I am concerned, an examination has no other purpose beyond that.

I never have had any idea of what a grade means on an individual's academic transcript. Now, since the person's work was probably done in collaboration with others, including me, my ignorance of the meaning of a grade is even more pronounced.

For instance, after reading a draft of this paper, my wife said, "Would you want to be operated on by a medical doctor who received an A on an examination during which he or she received a lot of help? How would you know whether he actually knows the location of the appendix he ostensibly is going to remove from your rather ample gut? He may not know an appendix from an earlobe." An astute person might correctly surmise that she is not exactly a supporter of the idea. Removing any doubt, she continued, "If the person who really knows the difference between an appendix and an earlobe—the real A student who gave your surgeon help on exams during their 'groupy' days of medical school—is not there to provide similar assistance, you are going to look funny when your hat slips down around your neck because your ear is missing. How would you like that?" My knee-jerk response—born of years of defining honor as the process of being unhelpful to others—was, "I wouldn't." But then I realized that she based those fearful questions on the identical knee-jerk assumptions. By redefining the assumptions, I think the question becomes, "How would you like to have surgery performed by a physician who has learned to solve surgical problems in the most effective manner, even if that means collaborating with others?"

The Bottom Line

Let's cut through to the most crucial issue: Does the system based on my new definition of cheating prepare students for the world of work?

I have reached the unequivocal conclusion that it does not. But as I mentioned before, I do think that it prepares them to do real work. There is a difference. After graduation, many of us become employees of phrog farms, where we seldom get rewarded for how well we sing in the chorus.

More profoundly, is it the function of business professors to certify students as competent carriers of anaclitic depression so that they can comfortably take their places in the swamps? Or, alternatively, is it to certify that both students and faculty have been provided an altruistic environment in which they can learn to perform real work and live real lives to the best of their abilities?

Again, the question is not trivial. For instance, a colleague has asked, "What happens to the certification process? A part of the value of education is providing some assurance that the person has gained some knowledge and skills. With the new rules, the certification process becomes only one of competency in eliciting help. Would a university remain viable once this became known?"

Although I think that the "new rules" make the certification process even more complicated than the question implies, I certainly believe that my colleague is asking the right questions. I know that they are the kinds of questions that have both plagued and stimulated me.

As you might guess, I have answered some of those questions for myself by concluding that for me to be competently ethical, I must try to provide not an echo but a choice, even if the choice is made on the basis of beliefs and values whose viability is not assuredly known. More specifically, if we should choose to adopt the new definition of cheating on a massive scale, I doubt that universities, as we know them, would remain viable. On the basis of my experiences thus far, though, I believe that universities as we *don't* know them would become even more viable. For me, that exploration of what we don't know would offer a rich opportunity for spiritual growth, intellectual stimulation, and much relief.

Rays of Hope

Although I don't sense any burgeoning desire on the part of professional educators to provide that choice, I do see a groundswell of hope being offered by the students whom they ostensibly teach but from whom they have much to learn.

For instance, the University of Delaware recently published a study that indicated that at least one-third of its undergraduate students had engaged in forms of cheating that involved giving and receiving aid.[17] The study also indicated that the data from that institution were similar to those reported by other institutions of higher learning. Furthermore, it reported that the percentage of students cheating in institutions of higher education has steadily increased over the past forty years.

However, my redefinition should not be dismissed as an effort merely to legitimize an irrepressible vice. Nor should it be seen as cynical surrender to deceit or trickery in commerce. Quite the opposite—I consider my redefinition to be an impassioned plea for business ethics. Those of us who are committed to the proposition that it is important to train our young in the skills of anaclitic depression, marasmus, and lonely individuality will look upon the Delaware data with alarm. Those of us who are committed to the proposition that it is important to train our young in the skills of altruism, community building, and synergy will see those same data as bright rays of hope. Seeing the data as rays of hope, I personally believe that it is the ethical and moral responsibility of those who educate our future leaders and followers to nourish that hope.

As far as I am concerned, failure to provide such nourishment would further educate our students in the pursuit of marasmic loneliness and would thereby make an important contribution to carrying me, you, them, and the culture as a whole to the breaking point. I don't think many of us want to do that. I know I don't.

If we do fulfill what I believe to be our moral and ethical responsibilities by encouraging students to cheat, then someday our grandchildren may be signing honor codes in which they pledge, "On my honor as a student, I certify that I have both given and received aid on this assignment." If that happens partly because business educators have championed the effort, then I believe that we can be justly proud of our contribution to the culture's growth and survival.

Notes

Chapter 1 – Introduction

1. Thomas Merton, *Raids on the Unspeakable* (New York: New Directions, 1966).
2. Jerry Harvey, "The Abilene Paradox," *Organizational Dynamics*, Summer 1974, 64–83.
3. Jerry Harvey, "Organizations as Phrog Farms," *Organizational Dynamics*, Spring 1977, 15–23.
4. Wilfred Bion, *Attention and Interpretation* (New York: Basic Books, 1970).
5. Robert Frost, *In the Clearing* (New York: Holt, Rinehart and Winston, 1979). Reprinted by permission.
6. Carl Jung, *Memories, Dreams, Reflections,* ed. Aniela Jaffe (New York: Pantheon Books, 1963).

Chapter 2 – The Abilene Paradox: The Management of Agreement

1. Editorial, "Watergate: The Painful Puzzle of Why." *Washington Star and Daily News.* 27 May, 1973. E1.
2. William Greider, "Loyalty Over Conscience: Nixon Aide Tries to Explain Why," *Washington Post*, 8 June 1973, A20. Reprinted with permission of *The Washington Post.*
3. "Text of Jeb Stuart Magruder Testimony Before the Senate Select Watergate Committee," *Washington Post*, 15 June 1973, A14.
4. Ibid.
5. Anatol Rapaport and Albert Chammah, *The Prisoner's Dilemma* (Ann Arbor: University of Michigan Press, 1970).
6. William Shakespeare, *Hamlet*, act 3, sc. 2. *The Tragedy of Hamlet, Prince of Denmark* (New York: Airmont Publishing Inc., 1965).
7. Charles P. Snow, *Two Cultures: And a Second Look* (London: Cambridge University Press, 1959), 6.
8. Tannenbaum, Robert, "Organizational Change Has to Come Through Individual Change." *Innovation.* No. 23 (August, 1971):36–43.
9. William Greider, "The Lost Sheep . . . Magruder's Sincerity Praised," *Washington Post*, 15 June 1973, A16.
10. Snow, *Two Cultures*, 6.

Chapter 3 — Organizations as Phrog Farms

1. Amanda Vesey, *The Princess and the Frog* (New York: Atlantic Monthly Press, 1985).
2. Frederick Herzberg, "One More Time: How Do You Motivate Employees?" *Harvard Business Review* 46 (January–February 1968):53–62.
3. Alfred Marrow, *Making Waves in Foggy Bottom* (Washington, D.C.: NTL Institute, 1974).
4. Hannah Arendt, *Eichmann in Jerusalem: A Report on the Banality of Evil* (New York: Viking, 1976). Copyright © 1963, 1964 by Hannah Arendt. All rights reserved. Reprinted by permission of Viking Penguin Inc.
5. R.D. Laing, *The Divided Self* (New York: Pelican Books, 1965).

Chapter 4 — Management and the Myth of Abraham; or, Go Plant a Cabbage on God's Behalf

1. *The Living Bible (Paraphrased)* (London: Tyndale House, 1971).
2. James H. Boren, *When in Doubt, Mumble: A Bureaucrat's Handbook* (New York: Van Nostrand Reinhold, 1972).
3. Robert Bretall, *A Kierkegaard Anthology* (New York: Modern Library, 1946).
4. Carl Jung, *The Portable Jung*, ed. Joseph Campbell (New York: Viking Press, 1971).
5. Erich Fromm, *Escape from Freedom* (New York: Holt, Rinehart and Winston, 1969).

Chapter 5 — Captain Asoh and the Concept of Grace

1. John J. Fialka, "Can the U.S. Army Fight? . . . The Officers Do More in the Volunteer Army," *Washington Star*, 19 December 1980, 1.
2. Ibid.
3. *Harper's Bible Dictionary*, ed. Paul Achtemeir (San Francisco: Harper & Row, 1985), 357.
4. National Transportation Safety Board, *Aircraft Accident Report: Japan Air Lines Co., Ltd. DC-8-62, JA80325* (Washington, D.C.: Bureau of Aviation Safety, 31 December 1969).
5. Rod MacLeish, "The Fine Art of Apology," *Washington Star*, 10 January 1981, A11.
6. Sissela Bok, *Lying: Moral Choice in Public and Private Life* (New York: Pantheon Books, 1978), 8.
7. Ibid., 132.
8. Cambridge Survey Research, 1975 and 1976, cited in ibid., xviii.
9. Charles Peters, "Would Carter Ever Lie About His Pulse Rate?" *Washington Post*, 17 June 1979, B8.

10. William Berkeley, "To Some at Harvard, Telling Lies Becomes a Matter of Course," *Wall Street Journal*, 15 January 1979, 1.

11. Wilfred Bion, *Attention and Interpretation* (New York: Basic Books, 1970).

12. Chris Argyris, *Intervention Theory and Method* (Reading: Mass.: Addison-Wesley, 1970).

13. Rene A. Spitz, "Hospitalism: A Follow-up Report," in *Psychoanalytic Study of the Child*, Vol. 2 (New Haven: Yale University, 1946).

14. George Vaillant, *Adaptation to Life* (Boston: Little, Brown, 1977).

15. "Anatomy of an Illness (as Perceived by the Patient)," *New England Journal of Medicine* 295(1976):1458–63.

16. Michael Maccoby, *The Gamesman: The New Corporate Leader* (New York: Simon and Schuster, 1976).

17. Argyris, *Intervention Theory and Method*.

18. Vaillant, *Adaptation to Life*, 110.

19. Edmund Wilson, *On Human Nature* (Cambridge: Harvard University Press, 1978).

Chapter 6 – Eichmann in the Organization

1. Hannah Arendt, *Eichmann in Jerusalem: A Report on the Banality of Evil* (New York: Viking, 1976). Copyright © 1963, 1964 by Hannah Arendt. All rights reserved. Reprinted by permission of Viking Penguin Inc.

2. Ibid., 175.

3. Ibid.

4. Ibid., 14.

5. Ibid., 25.

6. Ibid., 16.

7. Ibid., 131.

8. Bruno Bettelheim, "Individual and Mass Behavior in Extreme Situations," *Journal of Abnormal and Social Psychology* 38(1943):417–52.

9. Jules Feiffer, *Little Murders* (New York: Penguin Books, 1983).

10. Elliott Jaques, *A General Theory of Bureaucracy* (New York: Halstead, 1976).

11. Stanley Milgram, *Obedience to Authority* (New York: Harper Colophon Books, 1969).

12. Arendt, *Eichmann*, 105.

13. Ibid., 109.

14. Ibid., 11.

15. Halle, Kay. *The Irrepressible Churchill*. (New York: Facts on File Publications, 1985), 133. Copyright © 1966, 1985 by Kay Halle. Reprinted with permission of Facts On File, Inc., New York.

16. Arendt, *Eichmann*, 117.

17. Ibid., 218.

18. Ibid., 119.

19. Herbert A. Striner, "Economic Health Requires Investing in Labor Force," *Washington Star*, 6 February 1981, A12.
20. Ibid.
21. Arendt, *Eichmann*, 85.
22. Priscilla Meyer, "No More Nice Guy: Traditionally Paternal Equitable Life Rattles Staff by Mass Firings," *Wall Street Journal*, 11 December 1978, 1.
23. Leo, John. "Cleansing the Mother Tongue: Wanda Updates Ralph on Orgies, Frigidity and One Night Stands," *Time*, 27 December 1982, 78.
24. George Vaillant, *Adaptation to Life* (Boston: Little, Brown, 1977).
25. Arendt, *Eichmann*, 59.
26. Meyer, "No More Nice Guy."
27. Arendt, *Eichmann*, 91.
28. Ibid.
29. Ibid.
30. Ibid., 119.
31. Ibid., 127.
32. Laurence Shames, "Crimes of Silence," *Esquire*, June 1982, 19–21.
33. Arendt, *Eichmann*, 119.
34. Walter Clark, *The Ox-Bow Incident* (New York: Signet Classics, 1940).
35. Arendt, *Eichmann*, 82.
36. Sissela Bok, *Lying: Moral Choice in Public and Private Life* (New York: Pantheon Books, 1978), 13.
37. Arendt, *Eichmann*, 52.
38. Ibid., 119.
39. Meyer, "No More Nice Guys."
40. Barker, Karlyn. "U.S. Workers Facing RIF Get Little Aid. *Washington Post*, 9 September 1981, A1. Reprinted with permission of *The Washington Post*.
41. Wilfred Bion, *Attention and Interpretation* (New York: Basic Books, 1970).
42. Arendt, *Eichmann*, 12.
43. Ibid., 175.
44. William Ouchi, *Theory Z* (Reading, Mass.: Addison-Wesley, 1981).
45. Arendt, *Eichmann*, 106.
46. James Lynch, *The Broken Heart: The Medical Consequences of Loneliness* (New York: Basic Books, 1977).
47. Arendt, *Eichmann*, 32.
48. Ibid., 40.
49. George M. Kren and Leon H. Rappoport, *The Holocaust and the Crisis of Human Behavior* (New York: Holmes and Meier, 1980), 77.
50. Ibid., 108.
51. Arendt, *Eichmann*, 124.
52. Ouchi, *Theory Z*.
53. Philip Slater, *The Pursuit of Loneliness: American Culture at the Breaking Point* (Boston: Beacon Press, 1970).

54. Rowen, Hobart. "Management: Family Affair, Japan Tells U.S. Firms, *Washington Post*, 12 April 1981, G20.

55. Ibid.

56. Johnny Paycheck, "Take This Job and Shove It, I Ain't Working Here No More," Epic Records (Columbia), 1978.

57. Jaques, *General Theory*, 190–91.

58. Edmund Wilson, *On Human Nature* (Cambridge: Harvard University Press, 1978), 149.

59. Vaillant, *Adaptation to Life*, 110.

60. "Furloughs: Long Days, Short Morale," *Fairfax Journal*, 11 March 1982.

61. "A&P Workers Agree to Wage Cuts," *Washington Post*, Washington Business section, 20 December 1982, 9.

62. Arendt, *Eichmann*, 171.

63. Ouchi, *Theory Z*, 1981.

64. Richard T. Pascale and Anthony G. Athos, *The Art of Japanese Management* (New York: Simon and Schuster, 1981).

65. Thomas Rohlen, *For Harmony and Strength: Japanese White-Collar Organization in Anthropological Perspective* (Berkeley: University of California Press, 1974).

Chapter 7 – The Gunsmoke Phenomenon

1. Sigmund Freud, *Totem and Taboo*, trans. James Stackey (New York: Norton, 1950).

2. Solomon Asch, *Social Psychology* (Englewood Cliffs, N.J.: Prentice-Hall, 1952).

3. Wilfred Bion, *Experiences in Groups* (New York: Basic Books, 1961).

4. Irving Janis, *Victims of Groupthink* (Boston: Houghton Mifflin, 1972).

5. Jerry Harvey, "Type of Influence, Magnitude of Discrepancy, Degree of Dogmatism as Determinants of Conformity Behavior," Unpublished doctoral dissertation (Austin: University of Texas, 1963).

6. Asch, *Social Psychology*, 450–501.

7. Janis, *Victims of Groupthink*.

8. Leon Salzman, *The Obsessive Personality* (New York: Science House, 1968), 274.

9. *Time*, "The Battle over Bureaucracy." 6 March 1978, 13.

10. Eugene T. Mallove, "Einstein's Intoxication with the God of the Cosmos," *Washington Post*, 22 December 1985, C4.

Chapter 8 – Encouraging Future Managers to Cheat

1. *Academic Fraud and the Honor System* (Charlottesville: University of Virginia, undated).

2. Henry Mintzberg, *The Nature of Managerial Work* (New York: Harper & Row, 1973).

3. Peter Vaill, "Toward a Behavioral Description of High-Performing Systems," In McCall, Morgan et al., *Leadership: Where Else Can We Go?* (Durham, N.C.: Duke University Press, 1978), 111.
4. Chris Argyris and Donald A. Schon, *Organizational Learning: A Theory of Action Perspective* (Reading, Mass.: Addison-Wesley, 1978).
5. George Vaillant, *Adaptation to Life* (Boston: Little, Brown, 1977), 386.
6. Ibid., 110.
7. Ibid., 385.
8. Ibid., 110.
9. Hans Selye, *Stress Without Distress* (New York: Signet Books, 1974), 5.
10. Ibid., 73.
11. Edmund Wilson, *On Human Nature* (Cambridge: Harvard University Press, 1978), 149– 50.
12. Rene A. Spitz, "Hospitalism: A Follow-up Report," in *Psychoanalytic Study of the Child*, Vol. 2 (New Haven: Yale University, 1946).
13. James Lynch, *The Broken Heart: The Medical Consequences of Loneliness* (New York: Basic Books, 1977).
14. Philip Slater, *The Pursuit of Loneliness: American Culture at the Breaking Point* (Boston: Beacon Press, 1970).
15. Jerry Harvey, "Class Syllabus: Individual and Group Dynamics" (Washington, D.C.: George Washington University, 1983).
16. Barry Farber, "The Loneliness of the Burnt-Out Teacher," *Psychology Today*, July 1982, 28– 29.
17. Carol Pemberton, "Results from the Spring 1983 Student and Faculty Surveys on Academic Honesty at the University of Delaware," Institutional Research Study 83– 32 (Newark: University of Delaware, 1983).

Selected Readings

Chapter 1 – Introduction

Arendt, H. *Eichmann in Jerusalem: A Report on the Banality of Evil.* New York: Viking, 1976.

Becker, E. *The Denial of Death.* New York: Free Press, 1973.

Bion, W.L. *Experiences in Groups.* New York: Basic Books, 1961.

Harvey, J. "OD as a Religious Movement." *Training and Development Journal,* March 1974, 24–27.

Levinson, D.; Darrow, Charlotte; Klein, Edward; and McKee, Braxton. *The Seasons of a Man's Life.* New York: Knopf, 1978.

Chapter 2 – The Abilene Paradox: The Management of Agreement

Argyris, C. *Intervention Theory and Method: A Behavioral Science View.* Reading, Mass.: Addison-Wesley, 1970. An excellent description of the process of "owning up" and being "open," both of which are major skills required for assisting one's organization in avoiding or leaving Abilene.

Camus, A. *The Myth of Sisyphus and Other Essays.* New York: Vintage Books, Random House, 1955. An existential viewpoint for coping with absurdity, of which the Abilene Paradox is a clear example.

Harvey, J.B., and Albertson, R. "Neurotic Organizations: Symptoms, Causes and Treatment," Parts I and II. *Personnel Journal,* September and October 1971. A detailed example of a third-party intervention into an organization caught in dilemmas.

Janis, I. *Victims of Groupthink.* Boston: Houghton Mifflin, 1972. An alternative viewpoint for understanding and dealing with many of the dilemmas described in "The Abilene Paradox." Specifically, many of the events that Janis describes as examples of conformity pressures (that is, group tyranny), I would conceptualize as mismanaged agreement.

Slater, P. *The Pursuit of Loneliness.* Boston: Beacon Press, 1970. An in-depth description of the impact of the role of alienation, separation, and loneliness (major contributors to the Abilene Paradox) in our culture.

Toffler, A. *Future Shock* (New York: Bantam Books, 1970).

Walton, R. *Interpersonal Peace-making: Confrontation and Third Party Consultation*. Reading, Mass.: Addison-Wesley, 1969. A variety of approaches for dealing with conflict when it is real, rather than phony.

Chapter 3 – Organizations as Phrog Farms

Arendt, H. *Eichmann in Jerusalem*. New York: Viking, 1976. A terrifying discussion of the potential evil of swamp-bound organizations.

Bion, W.L. *Experience in Groups*. New York: Basic Books, 1961. A penetrating discussion of the manner in which groups and organizations pursue courses of action that subvert their essential purposes.

Herzberg, F. "One More Time: How Do You Motivate Employees?" *Harvard Business Review* 46 (January – February 1968:53 – 62. A generic differentiation between rape and seduction as it applies to motivation in an organizational setting.

Laing, R.D. *The Divided Self*. Baltimore: Pelican Books, 1965. Description of the impact of depersonalization.

Rapoport, A., and Chammah, A. *The Prisoner's Dilemma*. Ann Arbor: University of Michigan Press, 1970. An excellent discussion of zero-sum and non-zero-sum attitudes.

Finally, after skimming *Bartlett's Familiar Quotations*, I am intrigued by the way in which frogs have long played an important part in literature and mythology. Authors from Goethe to Mark Twain have made noteworthy references to frogs in their works, and in those references, frogs have ultimately served some serious purpose. Perhaps one ancient poet (Bion) spoke for all phrogologists when he said: "Though boys throw stones at frogs in sport, the frogs do not die in sport, but in earnest."

Chapter 4 – Management and the Myth of Abraham; or, Go Plant a Cabbage on God's Behalf

Abrahamsen, D. *Confessions of Son of Sam*. New York: Columbia University Press, 1985.

Boren, J. *When In Doubt, Mumble: A Bureaucrat's Handbook*. New York: Van Nostrand Reinhold, 1972.

Bretall, R. *A Kierkegaard Anthology*. New York: Modern Library, 1946.

Campbell, J. (ed.). *The Portable Jung*. New York: Viking, 1971.

Fromm, E. *Escape from Freedom*. New York: Holt, Rinehart and Winston, 1969.

The Living Bible (Paraphrased). London: Tyndale House, Publishers, 1971.

Lowrie, W. *A Short Life of Kierkegaard.* Princeton, N.J.: Princeton University Press, 1970.

Myers, I.B. (with P. Myers). *Gifts Differing.* Palo Alto: Calif.: Consulting Psychologists Press, 1980.

Chapter 5 – Captain Asoh and the Concept of Grace

Argyris, C. *Intervention Theory and Method.* Reading, Mass.: Addison-Wesley, 1970.

Berkeley, W. "To Some at Harvard, Telling Lies Becomes a Matter of Course." *Wall Street Journal,* 15 January 1979, 1.

Bion, W.L. *Attention and Interpretation.* New York: Basic Books, 1970.

Bok, S. *Lying, Moral Choice in Public and Private Life.* New York: Pantheon Books, 1978.

Bolman, L., and Deal, T. *Modern Approaches to Understanding and Managing Organizations.* San Francisco: Jossey-Bass, 1984.

Cousins, N. "Anatomy of an Illness" (as Perceived by the Patient)." *New England Journal of Medicine* 295 (1976):1458–63.

Early, P. "Hotel Employee Union Ratifies New Pact." *Washington Post,* 18 September 1981, B1.

Harper's Bible Dictionary, ed. P. Achtemeir. San Francisco: Harper & Row, 1985.

Maccoby, M. *The Gamesman: The New Corporate Leader.* New York: Simon and Schuster, 1976.

National Transportation Safety Board. *Aircraft Accident Report: Japan Air Lines Co., Ltd. DC–8–62, JA8032.* Washington, D.C.: Bureau of Aviation Safety, 31 December 1969.

Spitz, R.A. "Hospitalism: A Follow-up Report." In *Psychoanalytic Study of the Child,* Vol. 2. New Haven: Yale University, 1946.

Vaillant, G. *Adaptation to Life.* Boston: Little, Brown, 1977.

Whiting, R. "You've Gotta Have 'Wa.'" *Sports Illustrated,* 24 September 1979, 59–62+.

Chapter 6 – Eichmann in the Organization

Arendt, H. *Eichmann in Jerusalem: A Report on the Banality of Evil.* New York: Viking, 1976.

Auden, W.H. "In Memory of Sigmund Freud." In *Selected Poetry of W.H. Auden.* New York: Vintage Books, 1970, pp. 54–57.

Barrett, W. *The Illusion of Technique.* Garden City, N.Y.: Anchor Books, 1978.

Bion, W.L. *Experience in Groups.* New York: Basic Books, 1961.

———. *Attention and Interpretation.* New York: Basic Books, 1970.

Bok, S. *Lying: Moral Choice in Public and Private Life.* New York: Pantheon Books, 1978.

Boren, J. *When In Doubt, Mumble: A Bureaucrat's Handbook.* New York: Van Nostrand Reinhold, 1972.

Bouvard, M. *Labor Movements in the Common Market Countries: The Growth of a European Pressure Group.* New York: Praeger, 1972.

Bowlby, J. *Attachment and Loss: Volume I, Attachment.* New York: Basic Books, 1969.

————. *Attachment and Loss: Volume II, Separation: Anxiety and Anger.* New York: Basic Books, 1973.

Clark, W. *The Ox-Bow Incident.* New York: Signet Classics, 1940.

Fromm, E. *Escape from Freedom.* New York: Holt, Rinehart and Winston, 1969.

————. *The Art of Loving.* New York: Harper & Row, 1974.

Hall, C., and Nordby, V. *A Primer of Jungian Psychology.* New York: Mentor Books, 1973.

Harvey, J. "I Can Always Get Day Work." *Consultants Communique* 3, no. 3(1975): 2–4.

Hayes, R., and Abernathy, W. "Managing Our Way to Economic Decline." *Harvard Business Review*, July–August 1980, 67–68.

Holmes, T., and Rahe, R. "The Social Readjustment Rating Scale." *Journal of Psychosomatic Research* 2(1968):213–18.

The Holy Bible, Revised Standard Version. Grand Rapids, Mich.: Zondervan, 1971.

Jaques, E. *A General Theory of Bureaucracy.* New York: Halstead, 1976.

Kren, G.M., and Rappoport, L.H. *The Holocaust and the Crisis of Human Behavior.* New York: Holmes and Meier, 1980.

Lynch, J. *The Broken Heart: The Medical Consequences of Loneliness.* New York: Basic Books, 1977.

Meyer, P. "No More Nice Guy: Traditionally Paternal Equitable Life Rattles Staff by Mass Firings." *Wall Street Journal*, 11 December 1978.

Milgram, S. *Obedience to Authority.* New York: Harper Colophon Books, 1969.

Ouchi, W. *Theory Z.* Reading, Mass.: Addison-Wesley, 1981.

Pascale, R.T., and Athos, A.G. *The Art of Japanese Management.* New York: Simon and Schuster, 1981.

Paycheck, J. "Take This Job and Shove It, I Ain't Working Here No More." Epic Records (Columbia), 1978.

Rohlen, T. *For Harmony and Strength: Japanese White-Collar Organization in Anthropological Perspective.* Berkeley: University of California Press, 1974.

Shames, L. "Crimes of Silence." *Esquire*, June 1982, 19–21.

Slater, P. *The Pursuit of Loneliness: American Culture at the Breaking Point.* Boston: Beacon Press, 1970.

Spitz, R. "Hospitalism: A Follow-up Report." In *Psychoanalytic Study of the Child*, Vol. 2. New Haven: Yale University, 1946.

Striner, H. "Economic Health Requires Investing in Labor Force." *Washington Star,* 6 February 1981, A12.

Vaillant, G. *Adaptation to Life.* Boston: Little, Brown, 1977.

Wilson, E. *On Human Nature.* Cambridge: Harvard University Press, 1978.

Chapter 7 – Group Tyranny and the Gunsmoke Phenomenon

Asch, S. *Social Psychology.* Englewood Cliffs, N.J.: Prentice-Hall, 1952.

Bion, W.L. *Experiences in Groups.* New York: Basic Books, 1961.

Freud, S. *Totem and Taboo,* trans. James Stackey. New York: Norton, 1950.

Harvey, J. "Type of Influence, Magnitude of Discrepancy and Degree of Dogmatism as Determinants of Conformity Behavior." Unpublished doctoral dissertation, University of Texas, Austin, 1963.

Janis, I. *Victims of Groupthink.* Boston: Houghton Mifflin, 1972.

Lao Tsu. *Tao Te Ching,* trans. Gia-Fu Feng and Jane English. New York: Vintage Books, 1972.

Mallove, E.T. "Einstein's Intoxication with the God of the Cosmos." *Washington Post,* 22 December 1985, C4.

Salzman, L. *The Obsessive Personality.* New York: Science House, 1968.

Chapter 8 – Encouraging Future Managers to Cheat

Argyris, C., and Schon, D.A. *Organizational Learning: A Theory of Action Perspective.* Reading, Mass.: Addison-Wesley, 1978.

Farber, B. "The Loneliness of the Burnt-Out Teacher." *Psychology Today,* July 1982, 28–29.

Hall, J. "Decisions, Decisions, Decisions." *Psychology Today,* November 1971, 51–56.

Lynch, J. *The Broken Heart: The Medical Consequences of Loneliness.* New York: Basic Books, 1977.

Mintzberg, H. *The Nature of Managerial Work.* New York: Harper & Row, 1973.

Pemberton, C. "Results from the Spring 1983 Student and Faculty Surveys on Academic Honesty at the University of Delaware," Institutional Research Study 83-32. Newark: University of Delaware, 1983.

Selye, H. *Stress Without Distress.* New York: Signet Books, 1974.

Slater, P. *The Pursuit of Loneliness: American Culture at the Breaking Point.* Boston: Beacon Press, 1970.

Spitz, R.A. "Hospitalism: A Follow-up Report." In *Psychoanalytic Study of the Child*, Vol. 2. New Haven: Yale University, 1946.

Vaill, P. "Toward a Behavioral Description of High-Performing Systems." In McCall, Morgan et al., *Leadership: Where Else Can We Go?* Durham, N.C.: Duke University Press, 1978, pp. 103–25.

Vaillant, G. *Adaptation to Life.* Boston: Little, Brown, 1977.

Wilson, E. *On Human Nature.* Cambridge: Harvard University Press, 1978.

About the Author

Jerry B. Harvey is professor of management science at the George Washington University, Washington, D.C. He is a graduate of the University of Texas in Austin, where he earned an undergraduate degree in business administration and a Ph.D. in social psychology.

A member of the International Consultant's Foundation, a Diplomate of the American Board of Professional Psychology, and a member of the O.D. Network, Professor Harvey has served as a consultant to a wide variety of industrial, governmental, religious, and voluntary organizations. He has also written a number of articles in the fields of organization behavior and education and is currently involved in the exploration of moral, ethical, and spiritual issues of organizations.

Made in the USA
Middletown, DE
03 February 2020